BARNET
THE TWENTIETH CENTURY

INCLUDING
FINCHLEY, EDGWARE
AND HENDON

JOHN HEATHFIELD & PERCY REBOUL

SUTTON PUBLISHING

First published in 1999 by
Sutton Publishing Limited · Phoenix Mill
Thrupp · Stroud · Gloucestershire · GL5 2BU

British Library Cataloguing in Publication Data
A catalogue record for this book is available from the British Library.

ISBN 0-7509-2096-3

Title page photograph: Descendants of the medieval warhorse, these magnificent shire horses continue to earn their keep even at the end of the twentieth century. They are a reminder, too, of the importance of the horse as the prime mover of goods and services into and out of London. It was to supply just these that our district was first cleared and cultivated, and eventually built over.

Acknowledgements

Books such as this reflect the past and present work and efforts of many people. For example, although most of the photographs are from our own collection, many of the originals from which they were copied were taken by unknown or untraceable photographers. We are greatly in their debt. However, we would like to single out James Barber, whose photographs of Hendon around the beginning of the twentieth century are particularly fine.

Special thanks are due to Pamela Taylor, Joanna Corden and Alison Condé of the Borough's Archive and Local Studies Department who have, as always, gone out of their way to be helpful and constructive. In addition we would like to thank Nicholas Benn, Graham Bird, PC World, Cadbury Schweppes, Jack Prime, Don Robbins, Messrs Wetherspoon and Derek Warren.

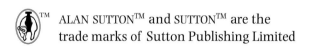

Typeset in 11/14pt Photina.
Typesetting and origination by
Sutton Publishing Limited.
Printed in Great Britain by
The Bath Press, Bath, Avon.

Contents

The London Borough of Barnet was created in 1965 following a Local Government Act. It was formed by merging the former urban districts of Barnet, East Barnet and Friern Barnet with the boroughs of Hendon and Finchley. There was considerable debate about the name to be given to the new borough, but after much controversy the decision was made to call it the London Borough of Barnet. There was much controversy, too, about the town hall for the new borough. It was decided, eventually, to use as the central portion the existing Hendon Town Hall which had been opened in 1901. This photograph, taken by E. Nicholls, shows the council chamber in 1952. Apart from extra seating, it is virtually unchanged today.

Introduction

No matter what our age or circumstance, change is always with us. It is part of life itself. And yet, how often do events pass by unnoticed or unappreciated until something occurs to bring them to mind? Who now remembers, for example, the passing of the old blue police boxes with their flashing light (made famous by Dr Who) that stood at most important road junctions in the borough, or the day the milkman's horse and cart was replaced by an electric float?

Many of the more significant changes, the ones that affect all of us, stem from national and international political decisions and advances in science and technology. The postwar National Health Service and various Social Security schemes, for example, transformed the health and well-being of the nation. Many older people in our area can recall the days before the era of mass vaccination and the discovery of drugs such as penicillin, when diseases such as TB, diphtheria, whooping cough and polio were often fatal. Those from poorer sections of the community can also remember when they could not afford the services of doctors and dentists, and so chronic illnesses and dental decay remained untreated. Worst of all was the threat of the workhouse at the end of their days. The idea of a medical service based on need rather than on the ability to pay was revolutionary and was not welcomed by most of the medical profession.

Not all changes have been for the better, however, and some have been a mixed blessing. Two world wars brought death and destruction to the people of our area but also hastened much needed social and political change. Although much of the area's considerable rural charm has disappeared under roads, houses and factories, the housing has been vastly improved. The motor car, which has transformed the lives of so many by giving them freedom and convenience of travel, has brought in its wake pollution, hopelessly congested roads and thousands of victims of road accidents.

Change comes about for many reasons, and it may be sudden or gradual. From the 1920s onwards radio and television transformed the lives of all classes. There are still people in the borough, for example, who saw some of the earliest aeroplanes take to the skies at Hendon and yet have lived long enough to see on their television screens a man land on the moon. On the other hand, there are many younger people almost overwhelmed by the speed of change of computers and information networks whose output and sophistication seems to alter week by week.

When we contemplate the benefits of what most people would regard as essential ingredients of modern living – the electric iron, vacuum cleaner and refrigerator, for example – a thought that often occurs is 'How on earth did people manage before the advent of this, that or the other invention?' Aside from the fact that many affluent people hired servants to do their menial work, almost always the answer is that they managed 'perfectly well'. The telephone is a good illustration of this point. As we approach the millennium, a feature of the streets, restaurants, public transport and even golf courses and motor cars is the number of people seemingly grafted to their mobile telephone. Today, it seems indispensable and yet for most people in the 1920s and 1930s its use was generally limited to the workplace, or hired for a few pence in a public call-box. Even earlier, around the turn of the century, people communicated perfectly well without a telephone. They used telegrams or handwritten postcards or letters which, if local, would often be delivered the same day they were posted. This system was sufficient for their requirements and adequate for their lifestyle.

The twentieth century, we are told, has seen more change than all other centuries put together. This book seems to confirm the truth of that assertion. What had formerly been sixteen rural and urban administrative areas were, by degrees, organised into larger administrative units culminating, in 1965, with today's huge London Borough of Barnet. And more changes are promised!

In 1901 the population of the combined area was about 76,000. Most of them would have been employed locally in domestic service or in agriculture, whose main crop was hay for the London markets. Jobs of any kind were in short supply and poverty was widespread. The 1991 census revealed a population of 294,000, 54 per cent of whom worked outside the borough and one-third of whom were employed in managerial or professional capacities. Although pockets of poverty exist, Barnet on the whole is an affluent borough.

Another important element has been the change in the ethnic composition of the borough. Apart from political refugees from Europe, most school photographs or registers taken before the Second World War indicate that there were very few people from other ethnic groups living in the borough. Historical events beyond the scope of this book changed the situation so that by 1991, the census records, 22 per cent of our residents were born outside the UK – 18 per cent of that number being non-white. The excellent race relations in the borough, while not perfect, are a tribute to all concerned and there is wide recognition of the resulting multicultural richness and diversity.

As the twentieth century draws to its close, it is clear that Britain's role in the world has changed profoundly. Gone are the Victorian pillars upon which its greatness was built. The Empire has long since disappeared and the country's vast wealth dissipated, not least by two world wars. For many people, Britain's very survival and prosperity may well depend on it being part of a larger European community. All these things, and more, have played their part in changing the face of the borough.

To record all such changes would be a massive task. Within these pages, therefore, we have featured those which seem to us of particular local relevance or to have unusual or interesting features. It is our hope that readers will be entertained and informed by our choice of subject and bask occasionally in a warm glow of nostalgia.

Chapter One
Transport

The 521 and 621 trolleybuses, such as the one shown here, ran from North Finchley to Holborn via Finsbury Park. They were introduced in 1938 to replace the 21 tram and were themselves replaced by buses in November 1961.

TRANSPORT

The Romans, with their incomparable engineering skills, built the first major roads to supplement the trackways and lanes used by earlier people. Part of today's Edgware Road was originally the Roman Watling Street which linked London with St Albans and beyond, and along it would have passed the military and civilian transport essential for the support of the Roman empire.

Another major road linking the capital to the north also crossed today's borough – the Great North Road, built in the early twelfth century. It ran originally through Muswell Hill, Colney Hatch, Friern Barnet Lane, Whetstone and on through Chipping Barnet. Sections of it were so bad in winter, however, that it was rerouted in the late thirteenth century to run from Highgate to East Finchley and across Finchley Common to join the original road at Whetstone. Along such roads would have passed riders and pack-horses, not to mention processions of people on foot. For the carriage of goods, large wheeled wagons were employed and by the middle of the seventeenth century stage-coaches began to make their appearance. Mail coaches, averaging around 8 mph, began to operate towards the end of the eighteenth century.

The poor state of roads led to the foundation of Turnpike Trusts which built and maintained roads from money derived by charging tolls from travellers. It was an unpopular but on the whole successful solution to the problem. In 1830, for example, a new turnpike road was opened which linked the west end of London with the Great North Road at Tally Ho!, North Finchley. The name Regents Park Road is a reminder of its intention. It ran through Childs Hill, where a toll-gate was erected, and on through Golders Green where another toll was collected at Hoop Lane. Yet another charge would be made at Whetstone. The coming of the canals and railways sounded the death-knell of the turnpikes which ceased to collect tolls by 1872.

The Railways

The railways were to revolutionise travel throughout Britain. In 1850 the Great Northern Railway Company built the first main line railway, from London to York. Colney Hatch (later called New Southgate) was one of the stations en route. In 1868 the Midland Railway built a line from St Pancras to Bedford with stations later called Hendon, Cricklewood and Mill Hill Broadway.

Branch lines soon followed and made it possible for wealthier commuters to travel daily to the City and elsewhere. In 1867 a line linked Finsbury Park to stations later called East Finchley, Finchley Central, Mill Hill East and Edgware. Another spur opened in 1872 which linked Finchley Central with Woodside Park, Totteridge & Whetstone and High Barnet.

With the coming of the London Underground, development of the area, including new concepts such as Hampstead Garden Suburb, proceeded apace. In 1902 the Underground Electric Railway Company obtained powers to extend the Charing Cross branch of its system (popularly called the 'tube') to Golders Green. By 1907 this was completed and the line was further extended by 1924 to the stations known today as Brent Cross, Hendon Central, Colindale, Burnt Oak and Edgware. The Barnet branch of the Northern Line was completed by purchase and subsequent electrification of the earlier steam train lines in the early 1940s.

Road Transport

The increasing population of the area needed more than railways to meet its travel needs. There was a growing demand for more road transport. In 1839, for example, only one daily coach ran from The Bell in Brent Street to Holborn. In 1856 two horse-drawn omnibuses ran from Barnet to London via Whetstone – a similar journey by the same method in 1870 took 1½ hours. By 1868 more local services were available: a horse-drawn omnibus, for example, ran from the railway station in Station Road, Hendon to Church End and beyond. Private cabs also ferried passengers from local stations to their homes.

It was the advent of the trams, however, which made local travel easier and cheaper for most people. By 1904 a tramway had been built along the Edgware Road which linked Cricklewood with Edgware. By 1905 a tramway linked Highgate and Whetstone; two years later it was extended to Barnet. By 1910 other routes served the district, including North Finchley to Wood Green via Friern Barnet and along Ballards Lane via Regents Park Road to Golders Green. The journey from Whetstone to Highgate, for example, took around 30 minutes and the fare was 3*d*; the first tram at 5 a.m. and the last at 11.12 p.m. Trams were replaced by trolleybuses from 1936 onwards. They were, in turn, replaced by motor buses which had served all the routes on a regular basis mainly after the First World War.

Transport also had a part to play in leisure activities. Cycling was a popular hobby in Victorian and Edwardian times and many people came from central London at weekends to enjoy the rural delights of the area. Motoring, too, became a popular pursuit but the huge growth in numbers of the motor car in recent years has presented both national and local authorities with one of their most intractable problems.

Matching the growth in importance of the motor car has been that of the aeroplane which has particularly early and close associations with the area. Aeroplanes were flying from Claude Grahame-White's Hendon Aerodrome as early as 1910 and aircraft of many types were made by him and by Handley Page at their Cricklewood factory. The aerodrome closed to flying in 1957 and it now houses the world-famous RAF Museum which opened in 1973.

East Finchley station, *c.* 1905. Note the platform sign which indicates the station was a stop for Hampstead Garden Suburb.

The change from horse-drawn hackney carriages to motorised licensed taxi-cabs and mini-cabs has been another development in public transport. Hackneys such as the one shown here outside Hendon (Midland) station plied their trade mainly between the station and the more affluent houses in the area.

In the early part of the twentieth century the local blacksmith was an essential part of the local economy. Apart from shoeing horses and repairing wheels of every description, he was called upon to mend just about everything made from metal. The more creative blacksmiths also made ornamental gates and fences. Walter Lines (wearing a traditional leather apron) ran the Old Forge Smithy in Whetstone's High Road.

The junction of Hendon Lane with Regents Park Road at the turn of the century. The dependence on the horse for transport is graphically illustrated. A tip-up cart, used to carry products such as sand and gravel, and a hay-cart wait to use the Metropolitan cattle trough. The horse-bus, by this time, permitted ladies to go 'outside' without offending modesty!

Cycling was a very popular pastime when this photograph was taken around the beginning of the century. By this time many bicycles had pneumatic tyres and were well built and reliable. All the

pride of possessing a good bike has been captured in this superb photograph taken by local Hendon amateur photographer James Barber. It features the Sneath family of Sunny Gardens Road, Hendon.

From 1904 onwards electric tramways began to appear on the main roads of many parts of the borough. Such was their popularity that new routes were rapidly introduced. Here we see a special tramcar testing a new section of route from Stanmore Corner (Canons Corner) in 1907. A mobile maintainance platform stands by in case further adjustments are required.

This photograph, taken from the tower of St John the Baptist's Church in Chipping Barnet in the early 1930s, shows the terminus for trams which was in use for over thirty years.

Newton's bicycle shop in the High Road, Whetstone, *c.* 1910. The Newton family's business prospered and they went on to open a successful garage near Station Road, Barnet.

Hendon's fire engine in 1909 was horse-drawn and powered by steam. On this occasion it had been called to a fire at Mill Hill School where the firemen were assisted by soldiers from the nearby barracks. At that time, on a 'good' day, the brigade might reach the scene of the fire in half an hour or so.

Hendon was one of the cradles of aviation in Britain. Hendon Aerodrome was founded in 1910 and soon became an important centre for the training of pilots, including those who would see action in the First World War.

Cricklewood Broadway, *c.* 1914. The Edgware Road, one of the main routes into London, was well served with buses such as those shown here. They were uncomfortable vehicles by today's standards. There was no windscreen for the driver, who relied upon special clothing for warmth and dryness in bad weather. Passengers on the 'outside' (i.e. the upper deck) fared little better.

With the coming of more reliable motor cars such as the Ford Model T shown here, motoring became an increasingly popular pastime and fewer and fewer horses were used for personal transport. Here, a member of the Busvine family poses with his mechanical treasure around 1919. The car stands outside the Busvine home, Woodhouse, which was later to become a grammar school and sixth form college.

The pub outing was a popular feature in the 1920s when this photograph was taken. Solid-tyred charabancs such as this one hired by the Black Bull at Whetstone, took their regulars on a day's outing to places such as Southend and Clacton. The luggage hold provided ample space for storing the crates of beer.

By the 1920s Newton & Son's garage near Station Road, Barnet, supplied the petrol, tyres, spares and repairs to meet an increasing demand. A breakdown vehicle, cleverly adapted from a car, was also on call for emergencies. The garage shown here was demolished in 1972 to make way for a block of flats.

Golders Green Road, 1920s. Change is in the air! A woman driver steers the latest sports car. The 84 bus route at that time went to St Albans via Ballards Lane, Whetstone and Chipping Barnet.

Finchley Central station in 1997. It still preserves a few architectural features from the original station that opened in 1867. The underground trains, unlike their steam-driven predecessors, have no classes of travel. The present rolling stock has been in use for some forty years; it is now obsolete and is currently being replaced.

The advent of the wheelie-bin in the 1980s heralded the appearance on the roads of an unusual vehicle, specially designed for a more mechanical system of household rubbish collection. The day of the traditional dustcart and metal bins had gone.

Some of the borough's roads are today among the busiest in Europe. This 1998 picture shows a quiet time at the junction of the M1/A1 near Copthall Stadium, Hendon. The huge lorries and trailers, many of them from mainland Europe, are to be seen at all hours of day and night.

Chapter Two
Entertainment & Recreation

The opening of Golders Green station in 1907 offered walkers and ramblers easier access to the rural delights of the area. It also encouraged property developers and businesses who, in a relatively few years, transformed the area with new buildings and roads.

ENTERTAINMENT & RECREATION

Before the introduction of railways and low-cost public transport made it possible for the man in the street to travel widely, most entertainment was local, centred around the village, hamlet and home. Religious holy days, although hardly entertainment, were celebrated in some style, as were more pagan festivals such as May Day, suitably adapted to make them respectable. Occasional visits from strolling players or similar entertainers would also enliven the local scene.

Barnet Fair and Other Events

Apart from the questionable delights of the local inn or beerhouse, perhaps the most eagerly anticipated local event of the year was Barnet Fair, established by charter of Queen Elizabeth I in 1588. People came from all over Britain to trade horses and cattle, as well as to sample the various side-shows and other entertainments. These included boxing booths. Boxing has long been associated with the Barnet area. Its proximity to London made it a popular venue for the illegal bare-knuckle fights that drew large, unruly crowds from the town and presented major problems to local magistrates and policemen in the eighteenth and nineteenth centuries. Matching, and often exceeding Barnet Fair in popularity, was the Welsh Harp – a large reservoir built in the 1830s to provide water to the Grand Union Canal. Throughout most weekends in the year, and particularly on Bank Holidays, large crowds came by train and omnibus to take part in the various activities, such as angling, boating, swimming, wrestling and rifle shooting. A nearby pub, in addition to the usual refreshments, offered its customers billiards, bagatelle and skittles.

Two other local events which drew the crowds were the Hendon Airshow and the Finchley Carnival. The flying displays started in 1912 and reached the peak of their popularity in the 1930s when the RAF organised the event. The Finchley Carnival started in 1900 and was originally staged to raise funds for the widows and orphans of local servicemen killed in the Boer War. Later, its profits were donated to the Finchley Memorial Hospital. The carnival was an instant success with hundreds of local traders and organisations taking part. Although the carnival still survives, it is a rather pale imitation of its former self.

Indoor and Outdoor Entertainment

The host of inventions and increasing prosperity of the late Victorian era gave rise to new types of entertainment. The piano, a common sight in many homes, was now supplemented by the early gramophone – a primitive device by modern standards – whose recordings were on wax or celluloid cylinders. It was now possible to dance and sing at home to music of a professional standard. In more affluent homes the formal 'musical evening', with refreshments and the guests contributing musical items or recitations, remained as popular as ever. Reports in newspapers of the time testify to the huge number of organisations which gathered in local halls throughout the borough and met the demand for debates, choral and photographic societies, lectures, flower shows and so on. Some of these societies were run by the local church or chapel and provided one of the few opportunities for boys and girls to meet. The Boy Scouts, Girl Guides and other youth organisations served the interests of the young, while bicycling clubs were a popular attraction for the more outdoor-minded. Local football and cricket teams, notably in Barnet, Finchley and Hendon, enjoyed considerable support from the local population.

Mass Entertainment – the Coming of the Cinema

The years just before the First World War saw the emergence of several types of mass entertainment venues. The first of these was the cinema, which has particularly close associations with our area. Birt Acres, one of greatest names in the invention of cinema-photography, lived and worked in Barnet and Hadley. Film studios also made their appearance. In 1913, for example, British Empire Films and Zenith Films opened an all-glass film stage at Woodlands, Whetstone. Although they specialised in filming stage productions from the West End, they also made short feature films, for which they would recruit local schoolchildren to play bit-parts. Payment was 6d a day with a cup of tea and bun thrown in for free during the afternoon. Later, Stoll Picture Productions founded their studio in the former aeroplane factory in Edgware Road; at the time, it was the largest film studio in England.

To cater for the demand for film shows, existing buildings such as skating rinks were adapted. Among the earliest cinemas were the Electric Palace in Cricklewood Broadway, which opened in 1911; the Old Bohemia (The Alcazar) located between Finchley's Princes Avenue and Redbourne Avenue – during the First World War this was converted into an observers' balloon factory; the Bijou in Brent View Road, Hendon, and what is today's Phoenix Cinema in the High Road, East Finchley, which is still screening films today.

By the 1920s and 1930s, with the change from silent to sound films, there was hardly a High Street anywhere which did not have its purpose-built cinema. Most of them had exotic names and many were remarkable architectural fantasies. Cinema was very big business with a few groups competing for the huge audiences. Some of the names of the cinemas are still with us – the Odeon, for example. Most have disappeared: the Ritz, Gaumont, Essoldo, Coronation, Bohemia, Athenaeum, Ionic, Classic, Bijou, Capitol, Regal and Grand Hall are among those remembered with affection by the older generation. Although the cinema survives, it could not compete with the arrival of television and the vast weekly cinema audiences are probably a thing of the past.

Theatre, Radio and Television

The district has been blessed with one first-class theatre: the Hippodrome in Golders Green opened in 1913 and closed in 1968, but in its time most of the great names of theatre, ballet and music trod its boards. It survives as a BBC theatre. In addition, a number of fine local amateur dramatic societies, among the best in Britain, have performed over the years in church halls and village halls to entertain thousands. Writing in 1981, Bill Gelder, doyen of local amateur theatre critics, observed that in thirty-three years he had reviewed well over a thousand plays for the *Barnet Press* – a remarkable testimony both to his stamina and the enduring popularity of this form of entertainment.

Radio was to rival the cinema in popularity. Like the cinema, it was a medium for mass entertainment but with one important difference: it entertained in the home. Television broadcasting started in the mid-1930s but its service was restricted to only a few viewers who lived near the BBC transmitter at Alexander Palace. Barnet was within that area, although relatively few people could afford to buy a television receiver with its tiny 9-inch screen. After the Second World War the service was revived and by the 1950s almost everyone was looking to purchase a set. Such was the popularity of television that most traditional forms of entertainment were badly affected, among them the weekly dances, radio, sports of all kinds, social clubs and outings. Many cinemas closed or were turned into bingo halls. As the millennium approaches, there is some evidence of a return to earlier forms of entertainment.

23

Barnet Horse Fair, 1905. The fair began in the sixteenth century and still exists today, although much altered. Its location has changed several times in its history. It was often a focal point for civil disturbance and crime, necessitating the drafting in of extra police.

Barnet Fair in the early years of the century when most of the machinery for roundabouts and other rides was powered by steam engines. Numerous side-shows included games of chance, so-called 'freak-shows' and the ever-popular boxing booth which offered small sums of money to anyone able to last three rounds with a resident professional boxer.

Friary Park, which opened in 1910, has always been a popular venue with young families. Tennis courts and a bowling green were later additions, as were a small boating pond and swings for the children.

Family tea parties and garden parties were popular events among the richer people. This 1905 photograph by James Barber shows Colonel Bacon and his family, who lived in Tudor House, Hendon.

A day on the Thames was a popular outing for many social groups such as those connected with churches, chapels, musical and debating societies. Featured here is a group from Hendon in the 1920s, when dress for such occasions was more formal than today's and hats were essential for both men and women. Notice the gentleman on the extreme right of the photograph who is pouring a cup of tea – a reminder, perhaps, that this was a 'respectable' teetotal outing.

By 1910, when this photograph was taken, the motor car was a convenient vehicle for 'a family day out'. With fourteen people travelling in just two cars this particular journey was probably not too comfortable.

Roller skating was a popular sport in the early years of the century and several special rinks were built. This is the Finchley skating rink next to the Swan & Pyramids, pictured around 1910. It had uniformed instructors and even a string orchestra but skating soon lost out to the attractions of moving pictures and the rink, like many others, was soon converted into a cinema.

Tennis has been, and remains, among the most popular of sports. Private clubs such as this one in Hendon were a popular and respectable meeting place for young people and were centres for much social activity.

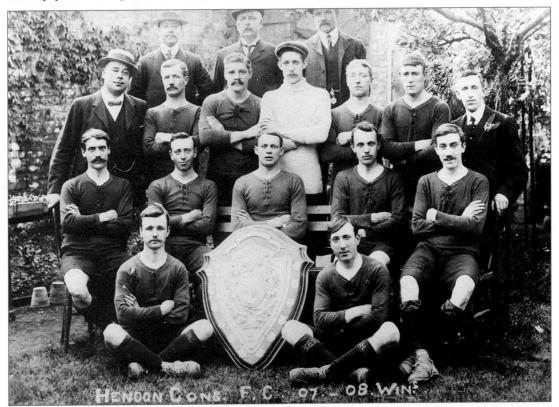

Football has been played in the borough throughout the century and long before. Amateur teams representing firms, villages and clubs were organised into local leagues for competitions and trophies. Today, the game is probably more popular than ever before, although the amateur aspect has long since gone for many senior clubs. The area includes one Football League team, Barnet.

The ladies of North Middlesex Golf Club, Friern Barnet, 1926. Most of them were married women whose husbands were also members of the Club.

In 1902 the great golfer Harry Vardon (seen here) was appointed professional at the South Herts Golf Club, Totteridge. He won the British Open a record six times and drew large crowds wherever he played. He died in March 1937 and a Blue Plaque marks his house in Totteridge Lane.

Henry Beach's Merit Motor & Cycle Works in High Road, Whetstone, pictured here in 1913, had originally been a smithy. He repaired motor cars, cycles, mail carts and even prams, and undertook to build bicycles to any design or specification.

The Finchley Carnival, 1907. The carnival was an extremely popular event which had been started in 1900 as part of a national campaign to raise funds for the widows and orphans of servicemen killed in the Boer War. Later, the money raised was used to fund the Finchley Memorial Hospital.

In the early years of the century it was not unusual to see the procession of animals from Lord George Sanger's Circus making their way along the borough's roads to their winter quarters in East Finchley. Sanger was a renowned showman who was murdered by one of his servants in 1911.

This artist's impression was used in a 1915 programme for the Bohemia Cinema on Ballards Lane, Finchley. The programme advertised the venue as having 'Winter and Summer Gardens; Vaudeville; Theatre; Ballroom; Concert Hall; Restaurant and Banquet Hall'. Its entertainment potential was overtaken by the demands of the First World War when it was converted into a factory making observation balloons. It was later replaced by the New Bohemia, also in Ballards Lane, which in turn was demolished to make way for today's Gateway House.

The Hippodrome Theatre in Golders Green opened on 26 December 1913. In its earlier years it was mainly a music hall but from 1922 until it closed in 1968 it also staged touring theatrical productions, orchestral concerts, ballet and opera. There was hardly an artiste of any note who had not, at one time or another, trodden its boards. The building survives and is currently used by the BBC for recording purposes.

Barnet Town prize band, 1906. The band was still going strong in the 1990s.

Amateur dramatic and operatic groups flourished (and continue to flourish) in many parts of the borough. This 1924 photograph shows members of the Mill Hill Operatic Society in their costumes for *The Mikado* by Gilbert and Sullivan.

Jack's Lake in Hadley Wood, *c.* 1935. The lake is a reminder that Britain's most popular sport is angling. At one time rowing boats could be hired by the hour.

A number of excellent open-air swimming pools were built in the years between the wars. The popularity of swimming is reflected in this 1935 photograph taken at the Mill Hill swimming pool. In fine weather the amount of time swimmers could spend in the pool had to be rationed.

Cricket in Sunnyhill Park, 1998. Public parks and open spaces administered by the borough are home to numerous sports activities such as cricket and football clubs. Bowls, tennis and children's playgrounds are other popular activities.

The first library in Finchley was opened in 1933 at Avenue House, East End Road. The growing demand for books saw a major expansion in the library service and in 1936 this branch library was opened in Ravensdale Avenue, Finchley. On its opening day it housed 10,000 volumes plus a small reference collection and the adult lending library and study room opened from 10.30 a.m. until 8 p.m. each weekday.

The rural nature of parts of the borough is reflected in this 1946 photograph of hounds and huntsmen leaving the yard of Bury Farm, Edgwarebury.

Chapter Three
Farms

Hollickwood, Friern Barnet, *c.* 1900. Haymaking was an essential part of
the local farming economy. It was labour intensive, thereby providing
some employment during the season. In the Middle Ages hay was cut
and gathered by hand, using scythes, rakes and pitchforks. Horse-drawn
reapers were introduced in the nineteenth century. The second operation
in haymaking, drying the hay, is complicated in England because the
weather is so uncertain, but as long as labour was cheap the hay could
be turned by hand for drying. Horse-drawn balers like the one shown
here were introduced into England from America at the Royal Show at
Derby in 1880 and spread rapidly. Silage-making is dependent on tractor
power and was introduced after 1960.

The estate was developed for housing in around 1935.

FARMS

In Roman times the district was extensively wooded. Some traces remain in place-names like Woodside and Woodhouse and physically in Scratch Wood, Coldfall, Hadley Woods and others. Over the centuries the trees were cut down for fuel and building purposes.

The agricultural and industrial revolutions of the eighteenth and nineteenth centuries and the area's close proximity to London led to a demand for hay. One notable person to capitalise on this was James Bridges (1674–1744), 1st Duke of Chandos, who obtained the contract to supply hay to the army. He bought large tracts of land in Hendon, Mill Hill, Barnet, Whetstone and Totteridge, and what was not already grazing land he speedily turned over to grass.

London's huge horse population ensured a steady demand for hay which was grown at the expense of other crops. The hay-carts carried the hay into London and returned laden with horse dung and soot for spreading on the fields. Although hay was still being supplied from Mill Hill in around 1920, the replacement of the horse by mechanical transport led to a rapid decline in this market.

Large estates, such as those at Canons, Edgware, Totteridge Park and Oakhill Park in East Barnet, included farms. Farms which have disappeared include Church Farms at East Barnet, Friern Barnet and Hendon, and Manor Farms at Old Fold Manor at Hadley, Frith in Mill Hill, Totteridge and East Finchley. A few farm names have survived in housing estates, including Gallants Farm, Courthouse, Goldbeaters, Dole Street, Coppets and Bittacy Farms.

By the 1920s the biggest threat to local farms came from developers buying up land for housing. Those farms that remained met the demand for local products. Small dairy farms supplied milk to customers within a 4 or 5 mile radius, while market gardens supplied fresh produce.

Faced with further growth in demand for housing land and competition from supermarkets, most small farms had gone out of business by 1970, although a few survived as garden centres or as riding stables. In 1999 College Farm, Finchley, the last surviving working milk farm, was itself threatened with closure.

Itinerant haymakers, Hendon, *c.* 1890. Gangs like this would travel from farm to farm getting in the hay crop and then moving on. The census returns show that many were Irish. They are recorded as sleeping in barns, lofts and even under hedges.

Haymaking at Barnet, *c.* 1900. The hay has been cut, raked and left to dry. The baler is on the left and the men on the right are loading the hay-cart. Notice the woman with a rake standing by.

The hog market, East Finchley, *c.* 1920. Around 1680 the George public house in Totteridge Lane was rented to the Odell family, who also kept pigs in three fields nearby. When the pub closed, they moved to East Finchley where they opened a hog market near the Great North Road. This eventually became one of the largest pig markets in the country. The whole area was destroyed by bombs in 1941.

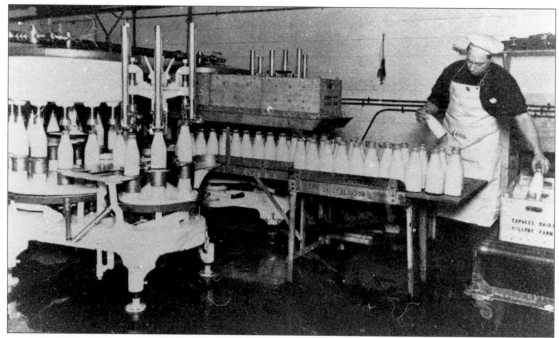

Bottling Plant, College Farm, Finchley. Glass milk bottles gradually replaced the traditional milk-can and churn in the 1930s. In the days before refrigerators were common, milk would go off in a few hours, so speedy delivery was essential and milk rounds were short. By the end of the century, milk was also sold in supermarkets in plastic containers.

Chapter Four
Housing

The White House, Downage, Hendon, 1999. This interesting house, designed by C.E. Simmonds, shows several features typical of the 1930s. The detached staircase on the left is made of reinforced concrete and embellished with a tall window. It is decorated with a winged motif. The porch roof, curved windows, round front door handles and tall chimneys on one side only are worthy of note. The house was described at the time as matching the innovative spirit of the 'Silver Jubilee' railway engine, the liner *Queen Mary* and the new television sets.

HOUSING

The oldest building in the borough is probably the undercroft of Totteridge Park, which is said to date from the thirteenth century. The house at 1266 High Road, Whetstone, is referred to in 1483 and has been restored by Pilgrim the builder. Other old houses include the rear of 1264 High Road, Whetstone (built around 1505), the Mitre pub in Barnet (1546) and Denham farmhouse in Totteridge (1550). There are some fine Georgian houses at Hadley, with others in Hendon Lane, Finchley, Wood Street, Barnet, Mill Hill and Totteridge. There are a number of almshouses in Hadley, Barnet, Friern Barnet, Hendon and Edgware, some dating from as early as 1613.

A number of factors contributed to the enormous growth of the population of England during the nineteenth century, including the discovery of asepsis, the introduction of clean piped water, the development of sewage systems and better diet. In the borough the population grew from 15,000 in 1851 to 76,000 in 1900 and to 115,000 in 1911. The population peaked in around 1951 when the figure was about 320,000.

The growth of the railways in Victorian times and the collapse of land values in the 1870s, provided the spur and the opportunity for developers to build new housing estates near the railway stations throughout the district. At first the fields near the railways stations were bought up. Terraces of small villas, built of yellow London Stock brick, were constructed in their thousands. Edgware, Hendon, East Finchley and Chipping Barnet all have many examples. Some were built down to a price, while others show detailed stone mouldings and others have little pieces of stained glass. Richer people had detached houses with separate accommodation for the obligatory servants and with carriage sweeps at the front and stabling at the side or rear. Examples include the Lyonsdown estate in New Barnet, Oakleigh Park in Whetstone, and later Bishops Avenue and Hampstead Garden Suburb. The large houses in Woodside Park and New Southgate were considered not to need carriage sweeps as they were built close to the station.

The enormous slaughter of the First World War was justified by stating that its purpose was to create 'a land fit for heroes to live in'. One result was the Housing of the Working Classes Act which caused local councils to increase vastly the number of cheap houses built for rent in the 1920s. The first council houses were built in Mays Lane, Barnet, in 1919, largely at the instigation of Councillor Olney. Other examples include the Russell Lane Estate in Whetstone (1921), Berkley Crescent in East Barnet, Ingle Way in Finchley (1926) and the Watling Estate in Edgware (1927/8).

In the 1930s the gradual recovery from economic recession was reflected in an increased demand for three-bedroom semi-detached houses built by a number of local firms including the Ideal Homes Company. The construction of the Piccadilly Line and other electric railways provided further opportunities for infilling. The Bethune Park and Ashhurst Road estates in Friern Barnet, almost the whole of Cockfosters and Deansbrook in Mill Hill all spring to mind. Purpose-built blocks of flats became common.

Though the borough suffered less bomb damage than many other parts of London, nevertheless some 42,000 houses were damaged or destroyed between 1939 and 1945. There were restrictions on new building in the immediate postwar period because the war had to be paid for, but by the early 1950s there was some postwar reconstruction, again mostly of local authority housing, like the East Finchley Market, Fordham Road, East Barnet and Dollis Valley estates. Some prewar plans were revived to complete the Mount Pleasant estate in East Barnet and the Woodside Park estate bordering Totteridge.

Land prices increased in the 1960s and various methods were used to increase the number of what were called 'housing units', usually by building blocks of flats including tower blocks, or by making rooms and corridors smaller. The 1960s and 1970s saw rapid price inflation, particularly of housing, sometimes by as much as 20 per cent in one year – and the introduction of 'gazumping'.

By the 1980s nearly all the available land had been used up and it became the practice to demolish Victorian houses with large gardens and build blocks of flats in the space. Though some of the early flats were cheap and nasty, by the 1990s developers were spending more time and money on design. As always England was class-conscious and the phrase 'executive housing' was invented to justify the high prices that new houses could command by the end of the twentieth century.

Hampstead Garden Suburb

Hampstead Garden Suburb was the concept of a group of remarkable people. Dame Henrietta Barnett (1851–1936) was born Henrietta Rowland. At the age of eighteen she came to London to help Octavia Hill and found employment as a relief worker among the poor of Marylebone. There she met and married Samuel Barnett, the local curate. One of the most remarkable women of her generation, her name is commemorated in the school.

Her colleagues included Sir Raymond Unwin (1863–1940), who was described as 'the father of English town planning', and Sir Edwin Lutyens (1869–1944), designer of the Cenotaph in Whitehall and the great memorial to the missing at Thiepval near the River Somme in France.

Above left: Mrs Holmes, wife of the local station master, at Hadley Road, New Barnet, *c.* 1926. The Lyonsdown estate developed steadily after the coming of the railway in 1851, with Cromer Road completed in 1910 and Sherwood Road around 1926.

Above right: The Holly Park estate in Friern Barnet covered 33 acres between the railway and Friern Barnet Road. There were few houses on the estate before 1871. The main estate was laid out as 424 plots by 1879, when sewers were laid in Beaconsfield, Glenthorne and other nearby roads. The houses – described at the time as 'pretty villas' because of their stone decorations – were largely completed by 1896. Estates consisting of houses like this followed the railway development all over the borough.

Left: Springfield Road, New Southgate, 1998. Not all houses in New Southgate were small villas. Larger houses and shops were built from 1870 onwards by G. Knight Smith (who lived in the house shown here) and other developers. Originally called Colney Hatch, the names of the district and the station itself were changed in 1876 in order to spare the 'embarrassment' of local residents.

Eastern Road, East Finchley, 1998. The roads off Fortis Green, East Finchley, were largely laid out by W. Collins, who lived at Fortismere, a large house at the Muswell Hill end of the road. They contain some of the most attractive houses in the borough. Many are double-fronted with bow windows.

Woodside Park, North Finchley, 1904. Woodside Park, on the borders of Finchley and Whetstone, displays the Edwardian fashion for pargetting at its peak. Built around 1904, the houses on the estate show a high degree of craftsmanship. The term 'Park' became very popular, implying social superiority, and is echoed in road names like Oakleigh Park, Torrington Park and Finchley Park.

Golders Green, 1903. The first house in Golders Green, shown here, was built on the corner of Hoop lane in 1903. The opening of the railway station and the development of Hampstead Garden Suburb were strong stimuli to development.

Hampstead Garden Suburb, 1998. The first sod in Hampstead Garden Suburb was cut here at 140/142 Hampstead Way. Originally of some 243 acres, the estate was enlarged by a further 730 acres, providing houses for about 11,000 people. The suburb was largely the creation of Henrietta Barnett, Raymond Unwin and Edward Lutyens.

Hampstead Garden Suburb, Central Square, 1998. Although the HGS Development Company provided some plots where buyers could employ their own architects, many chose designs by Lutyens, Unwin and their pupils. Sir Edward Lutyens designed St Jude's Church and the Free Church, the Institute and the south end of Erskine Hill.

Bishops Avenue, East Finchley, 1998. Bishops Avenue, near the border with Hampstead, was laid out for 'expensive houses' after 1897. The first residents included Robert Sainsbury and James Lyle, both provision merchants. Gracie Fields lived there in 1937. By 1999 there seemed to be a competition to build the most opulent house. This is one of the more modest dwellings. Electronic security gates are fitted to most houses in the road.

Totteridge, 1935. The Croft, Totteridge Green, was built around 1898 by T.E. Collcutt (1840–1924) for his own use. He also designed Fairspear (1899), Strathearn, West Lodge and the Lynch House (1904/5), all in Totteridge. In addition, he designed the decor for many P&O liners, the Town Hall in Wakefield, the Savoy Hotel in London (1889), the Palace Theatre (1890), the Imperial Institute in Kensington (1893), the Wigmore Hall and extensions to Mill Hill School (1907).

Totteridge, 1998. Lynch House, Totteridge Common, was designed by Collcutt in 1904 for Alexander Howard. They had met when Howard was awarded the contract to supply wood for fitting out the P&O liners. The house was named after the Lynch House in Kensworth near Dunstable, where Mr Howard was born.

Watling Estate, Edgware, 1998. In 1924 London County Council bought Goldbeaters Farm, Edgware, with 390 acres of land. At the time this was the largest LCC estate. Building began to the designs of the architect G. Topham Forest in 1927 and by 1931 some 4,021 houses and flats had been completed. At its height in 1937, the population on the estate was 19,012. A high quality of design is apparent in the mixture of tarred weatherboarded, brick built and roughcast houses. Special care was taken to retain the old trees and to create a rural atmosphere by building winding roads.

Whetstone, 1929. The Russell Lane estate in Whetstone was built for Friern Barnet Council. In March 1921 Messrs Walter Jones were awarded the contract to build the first forty-five houses on the estate for £30,805. The money was borrowed by the council at 6½ per cent for eighty years.

Vernon Court, Hendon Way, 1998. One of the first purpose-built blocks of flats in the district was put up in Hendon Way in 1927. This was an early example of ribbon development. No one at that time could have foreseen the rise of the motor car and the consequent parking problems. Amy Johnson, the pioneering woman aviator, lived here in 1931/2.

Edgware High Street, 1999. Another feature of the expansion of the 1930s was the building of terraces of shops with flats above, a development of the Victorian idea of the corner shop with the owner living on the premises.

Hollickwood Road, Friern Barnet, 1998. Described by the Ideal Homes Company as 'Britain's most popular house', three-bedroom semi-detached houses with garage space were built widely across the borough following the opening of the electric railways in the late 1920s and 1930s.

Deansbrook Road, Mill Hill, 1999. A new feature of the 1930s was the bungalow. Because they take up more ground than a conventional house, they could be built only in the suburbs where land was comparatively cheap.

Mill Ridge, Edgware, 1998. With the mid-1930s came a particular art deco style of design, demonstrated particularly well in the Astaire/Rogers films and reflected in houses with green pantiled roofs and with metal-framed windows often manufactured by Critalls. The little railed balcony is noteworthy.

Osidge Lane estate, East Barnet, 1998. With its flat roof, reinforced concrete porch cover and curved metal windows, this house is the epitome of the styles of 1936.

The former Market Place in East Finchley, 1998. Following extensive bomb damage in 1941, this region of East Finchley was completely rebuilt in 1954 and included eleven-storey blocks of flats, conventional houses, a play space, a youth club and a school.

Barnet Hill, 1998. The Dollis Valley housing estate lies at the foot of Barnet Hill. This futuristic concept was designed in 1965 by Lyons, Israel, Ellis & Partners, architects, and built on land belonging to Barnet UDC (formerly the sewage farm), at a cost of £1,705,950. It may be significant that none of the architects who designed these houses chose to live in them.

Vale Farm estate, East Finchley, 1998. In 1975, 274 flats were built here, with a further 109 houses built in Holden Road in 1977. The whole presents an attractive mix of houses and small blocks of flats.

No. 18 Oakleigh Park North, Whetstone, 1996. By the last quarter of the twentieth century nearly all the possible building land had been occupied and developers began demolishing older houses with large gardens and filling the sites with several smaller houses.

Ravenscroft Almshouses, Potters Lane, Barnet, 1998. Improvements in diet and medical care have meant that care of the elderly has become a growth area in recent years. Sheltered housing, such as this provided by the Ravenscroft Trust, is designed to meet that need.

Bruce Road, Barnet, 1946. Mr and Mrs Reeve with their daughter Georgina are pictured receiving the keys to the first pre-fab, in Bruce Road, Barnet, in April 1946 from Ted Offord, Chairman of Barnet Council. Pre-fabs were made from aluminium panels which were surplus from wartime aircraft production. They were at the forefront of contemporary design and were very popular with those who lived in them.

Chapter Five
Education

Copthall School, 1995. Copthall School was opened in Page Street, Mill Hill, as a girls' grammar school in 1936. Reorganised in 1976, it is now a genuinely comprehensive school for girls. Reflecting the rest of the borough, it enjoys a wide social, ethnic and religious mix. Schools must be one of the few organisations where Jews, Moslems, Hindus, Protestants and Catholics, not to mention pupils of other faiths and of none, can sit in the same room and hear and respect each other's views.

EDUCATION

Early Days

In Tudor times most children in the borough never went to school, and most adults could neither read nor write. When boys grew up, they usually worked at the same kind of jobs as their fathers. Girls and women generally stayed in the home.

In 1573 a 'common grammar school for the education, bringing up and instruction of boys and youth, for one master and one usher for ever to continue and remain', was opened in Barnet. Lessons were in religion and Bible studies, arithmetic, handwriting and Latin. At that time Latin was called Grammar, so the school was called Queen Elizabeth's Grammar School.

There was a school in the High Road, Whetstone, just south of what is now Atheneum Road, by about 1600. Probably also used as a chapel, it was called the bell house, because it had a bell. This school was accidentally burned down in 1662.

Ann Orme, a schoolmistress in East End Road, Finchley, died in 1704. There was a small charity school nearby from about 1719 until about 1785, although most Finchley children had no schooling. In 1815 it was said that 'no parish within 100 miles of London had more children in a deplorable state of ignorance' than Finchley. At about the same time, as a result, a number of church schools were built. St James' School in Friern Barnet Lane, for example, opened in 1810. There was a school at Church End in Finchley by 1813. St Andrew's School, Totteridge, opened in 1837, though there was a Nonconformist school in Totteridge Lane in 1828. Moxon Street School in Barnet opened in 1835. East Barnet received a grant in 1822 of £20 'towards the cost of fitting up a daily school for 56 boys and 56 girls'. The 'Truth' School in Edgware is a little later.

Hadley had three early schools. Hadley infant school was opened on the Green in 1835. It was paid for with monies originally invested in the South Sea bubble. There was another near Hadley Highstone and a third (which still exists) on the Common.

The Victorian Period

Education remained in the hands of the churches until the Education Act of 1870 made attendance at school compulsory. Children went to school at the age of five and attended for about seven years, usually leaving at twelve, but those who passed the Standard Seven test before that age left early. At the end of each year, pupils were tested to see if they were up to standard. If they passed, they went up a class; if not they stayed down to repeat the year. Teachers were paid according to results. Fees were charged until the abolition of the school pence in around 1890.

There was fierce resistance in the district, led by the then Vicar of St John's Church, Whetstone, to the idea of the state taking control of education away from the churches.

Local school boards were set up, initially for each parish, Edgware, for example, in 1875 and East Barnet in 1893. Control was later (around 1902) taken over by local councils. The money for the council schools came from the state. Schools offering more advanced courses for pupils staying until aged sixteen were also controlled by Middlesex County Council. Examples include Finchley (1905) and Hendon County Schools.

One of the many results of the First World War was the realisation that Britain lagged far behind Germany in the field of education. In 1926 the Hadow Report recommended the raising of the school leaving age for all to fourteen, with pupils transferring to separate schools at eleven. There were to be three kinds of school after age eleven: elementary schools for most pupils, secondary schools for those more academically minded and a new type of Central or Technical school. Because the latter would cost money to equip, disappointingly few were built.

After the Second World War

The 1944 Education Act embodied the ideals of secondary (that is, advanced) education for all. Pupils were to be tested at age eleven in order to identify the kind of schooling best suited to their needs. The notorious eleven-plus exam was actually invented as a method of helping pupils to identify those needs. New modern, grammar and technical schools were to be built. Social pressures, which identified grammar schools as 'better' and therefore classified those who did not get into them as 'failures', clouded a genuine attempt to create a fair system.

During the 1970s therefore, under the leadership of Councillor Vic Usher among others, the London Borough of Barnet adopted the comprehensive system whereby most pupils would go to their local school. The eleven-plus selection process was abolished.

By the late 1980s, political ideology caused the introduction of local management for the schools, removing control from the local authority and vesting it in the school's governing body. Because some schools are more popular than others, some kind of selection, with schools setting their own admission criteria, has been unavoidable. This has led to the partial dismantling of the comprehensive system, thereby causing more controversy and heartache.

By the early 1990s market forces and league tables were introduced with the intention of forcing schools to do better. Many responsible educational experts have serious reservations about this system. Perhaps the next millennium will show whether competition between schools really works.

Queen Elizabeth's Boys' School, 1935. Now Tudor Hall, Queen Elizabeth's Grammar School for Boys in Wood Street, Barnet, was founded by royal charter dated 24 March 1573. The school had outgrown Tudor Hall by 1932 and moved to purpose-built accommodation in Queens Road.

Queen Elizabeth's Girls' School, 1957. This is said to have been the first time that Queen Elizabeth II had visited a state school. She is pictured at Queen Elizabeth's School for Girls in Barnet with the then headmistress, Miss Freda Belson, on 17 November 1957. Alderman Harold Fenn, Chairman of the Governors, is next to the queen.

Trent School, 1961. Typical of many parish schools, Trent Church of England School in Cockfosters was opened in 1838. The school was completely rebuilt between 1956 and 1962 to the designs of Mr K. White, one of the governors of the school. The picture shows the 1838 building on the left with the 1956 replacement on the right. By 1999 there were about 210 children attending the school.

Deansbrook School, 1998. Deansbrook Junior School in Mill Hill was designed by W. Yates of Middlesex County Council architects' department in 1931 and was based loosely on the idea of an Oxford college with a central quadrangle. It cost about £7,000 to build. The nearby infants' school opened in September 1933. By 1999 the junior school had about 300 children on the roll. For the first sixty years of the century instrumental tuition in state primary schools was very rare. There was a huge increase in the 1970s followed by drastic cuts in the 1990s. By 1998 this junior school was one of only 8 per cent of English primary schools still offering instrumental music as part of the curriculum.

Sacred Heart RC School, 1998. The Sisters of the Sacred Heart took over a house in Oakleigh Park South, Whetstone, in 1936 and opened a private school for girls aged five to fourteen. Two other neighbouring houses were taken over in the 1940s. A dining hall was added in 1956, a teaching block in 1961 and an administration unit in 1971. In 1967 the school became a Voluntary Aided JMI school and the older pupils went elsewhere. By 1999 there were about 420 children on the roll.

Northside School, *c.* 1928. Percy Road School was the first school built by the Finchley School Board in North Finchley. It opened in 1884 and was designed to take 750 children. By 1898 it had been enlarged to accommodate some 930 pupils. The name was changed to Northside in 1932. The linked secondary modern school, called Hillside in 1955, moved to Summers Lane in 1956. By 1976 the primary school had about 470 pupils and by January 1999 about 420.

St Mary's C of E School, *c.* 1902. St Mary's School for 35 boys and 35 girls opened at Church End, Finchley, in 1813. By 1846 there were 67 boys and 32 girls being taught in two small classrooms. The school was relocated to Dollis Park in 1990. The site of the former school is now occupied by the local County Court.

Woodridge School, 1998. Woodridge School, Totteridge, was opened in 1967, though negotiations to build it had been going on since 1936. A bungalow building, it has a central hall and the obligatory kitchen and dining hall. School dinners are now such an essential part of school life that many extra-curricular activities would cease if the dinner hour were not available.

Christ's College, *c.* 1920. Christ's College in Hendon Lane opened as an independent school but ran into financial trouble in 1909. It was taken over by Middlesex County Council and became a grammar school for boys and by 1976 had 600 pupils. It was later amalgamated with Alder School.

Long Lane School, *c.* 1920. East Finchley Board School opened in Long Lane in 1884. It replaced an earlier school in Chapel Street. There were originally 500 girls, 500 boys and 350 infants in separate departments. By 1903 there were 1,200 children on the site. The school was reorganised in 1931 and renamed the Alder School. It became a secondary modern school in 1944 and was replaced by a comprehensive school called Brooklands in 1977. The building has been demolished.

Compton School, 1998. By the end of the twentieth century science was a core part of the curriculum. Accurate observation and recording are part of any scientist's training. The school was named after the Middlesex and England cricketer, Dennis Compton.

Compton School, 1998. Compton School in Summers Lane, Finchley, was the first purpose-built secondary school to be constructed by the new London Borough of Barnet. It replaced the former Manorhill School. The first intake of about 150 pupils came in 1992. The school had a budget in 1996 of about one and a half million pounds. Success in the sixteen-plus exams is widely regarded as the foundation of a good career.

Woodhouse Sixth Form College, 1998. The school opened in December 1922 and took the name Woodhouse in 1923. It became a grammar school under the 1944 Education Act. After the borough adopted the comprehensive system in 1975, the site was used as a sixth form college. In 1998 about 360 students took A level exams here.

Barnet College, 1998. Barnet College began life in 1896 as a centre of the London Society of the Extension of University Teaching, with a series of lectures on 'Some periods of English Literature'. Following the move of Queen Elizabeth Boys' School in 1932, the County Council bought the site with a view to creating a Technical Institute. The name was changed to Barnet College in September 1963. By 1999 the college had about 16,000 full- and part-time students, making it the largest educational establishment in the borough.

Hendon Technical College was opened in 1939. The architect was H.W. Burchett of the Middlesex County Council architects' department, a reminder of how talented the local authority staff were. There were substantial additions to the building in 1955 and a purpose-built engineering block was added in 1969. After having been a polytechnic, the buildings became part of Middlesex University.

East Finchley Youth Club, 1998. Wilmot Youth Club in East Finchley is named after Alderman H. Wilmot. The phenomenon of 'yoof' is a concept particular to the last half of the twentieth century. One of its first manifestations was the creation of purpose-built youth clubs in the 1950s, which gradually became less popular as television spread.

St Catherine's School, Barnet, 1998. Carol concerts, music festivals, folkdance parties, Empire days and half day holidays for Armistice day are all examples of the kind of activity that have gradually been crowded out of the curriculum as the century has moved on.

The nursery class, Whitings Hill School, 1998. In 1997 the new Labour Government was elected and pledged to provide nursery education for all three-year-olds whose parents wanted it. By 1999 Barnet Local Education Authority had provided places for about 2,755 children in forty-three nurseries and nursery classes staffed by some 126 adults, at the cost of about £3,808,750 a year.

A Barnet school in September 1939. Schools were an important part of the war effort. Teachers worked extra hours, dealing not only with gas masks and air raids and related matters but also helping with evacuation and releasing mothers to work in factories. By the end of the century the idea of the working mother with children at school had become commonplace.

Chapter Six
Pubs & Hotels

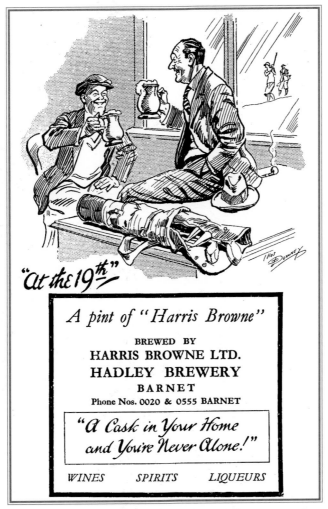

Newspaper advertisement, 1935. Because Hadley is situated on gravel soil, the local water is pure and so is particularly suitable for brewing. Hadley Brewery was operated by the Brown family from 1857 and was particularly noted for its ginger beer. The brewery supplied the nearby Folly Farm pleasure grounds which were a popular venue for Sunday School treats and excursions from Kings Cross. In 1938 it was taken over by Fremlins who used it as a distribution centre until 1974, after which it became derelict. In 1994 the buildings were demolished by Crest Homes of Weybridge who used the site for housing.

PUBS & HOTELS

Medieval water was not always of the purest quality, partly because raw sewage was normally discharged straight into streams and partly because earth privies were often dug near wells. Ale was widely drunk in preference to water.

Beer was often brewed 'in house'. An Assize of Bread and Ale, administered by the Lord of the Manor, controlled the quality of these goods, which sometimes was lamentably poor. In 1484, for example, the ale-taster reported that 'Thomas Sanney and John Doget are commonly accustomed to put les hoppez in their ale'. In 1610 William Miller of Hadley was fined for selling ale that was 'foul, loathsome and disgusting'.

Our district is particularly rich in the variety, number and historical interest of its pubs and hotels. This is in part due to its proximity to London to which it has been linked since early times by two main roads, the Roman Watling Street (today's Edgware Road) and the Great North Road (first referred to as such about 1694).

In the days of horse-drawn traffic the district, being about 10 miles from London, was a convenient first or last stop to change horses. Numerous pubs and hotels sprang up to meet the demands of these travellers.

The name of each pub might refer to political, religious or historical connections, the Kings Head being a popular choice. The Balfour Act of 1904 did much to control the number of pubs, while the two world wars played a part both in reducing the strength of beers and in controlling licensing hours. The award of an annual licence was dependent on satisfactory premises, standards of cleanliness and good organisation.

The growth of population between the two world wars led to the opening of pubs on the new housing estates, with opportunities for new concepts in pub architecture and decor. Pubs later came under the control of large brewing groups which had the necessary capital and expertise to exploit the growing market.

The last decade of the century saw further changes. There was a practice of changing the names of pubs so that they became a 'fashion statement'. The Red Lion at Barnet became the Dandy Lion. The Orange Tree at Friern Barnet became Big Hand Mo's. The decor reflected this trend, with a cocktail bar approach replacing the more traditional wooden beams and open fires.

In the last ten years the increasing cost of hotels in central London has encouraged major hotel groups to build new hotels. The nearby M1 and M25 motorways have motels at Scratchwood and South Mimms. One of the most striking changes, however, has been in the provision of food. 'Pub grub' has become popular and some pubs have quality restaurants attached.

The Old Bull & Bush, Hampstead, *c.* 1910. Famous in music hall song, the Bull & Bush is in the North End Road on the edge of Hampstead Heath. It served meals as well as drinks. When the Hampstead tube line extension to Golders Green was opened on 22 June 1907, free travel was offered and 14,000 people were said to have visited the Bull & Bush in one day.

The Hendon Hall Hotel, 1998. One of the district's premier hotels, Hendon Hall was once the home of the actor David Garrick. It is traditionally the overnight venue for teams visiting Wembley Stadium for the Cup Final and other international sporting fixtures.

The Bankers Draft, New Southgate, 1998. An interesting conversion, this former bank building was taken over by Messrs Wetherspoon for use as a pub.

The George Inn, Edgware, c. 1910. The old George Inn appears to be a Tudor building. It was one of the many coaching inns dependent on travellers using Watling Street. Note the horse trough outside the front door. However, it was not just the horses that were thirsty.

Chapter Seven
Shops & Shopping

Brent Cross shopping centre opened in 1976. It houses numerous shops and restaurants and is among the most popular and successful of its kind in Britain. An estimated 250,000 people visit the centre every week and its annual turnover is around £300 million.

SHOPS & SHOPPING

Few things reflect the changes of the last century more than the way consumer goods and services of every description are made and sold. We can only wonder what our ancestors would have thought about today's High Street with its garages, launderettes, betting shops, charity shops and DIY stores. Even more baffling would be the ubiquitous fast-food shops dispensing hamburgers, pizzas, doner kebabs and the like.

The small, compact villages of earlier times were largely self-sufficient, with any other requirements being bought or traded at the nearest weekly market. Towns would be supplied by small shops and stalls erected in the main roads. Annual fairs such as Barnet Fair catered for more ambitious purchases such as cattle and horses, their trading being enlivened by entertainments of every description. Today's markets, such as that at Chipping Barnet, are a reminder of those times.

Shops and stalls were not the only method of selling goods. Itinerant pedlars, such as the lavender girl and muffin man, supplied a wide range of products advertised through their individual street cries. Today's rag and bone men and costermongers are perhaps the last survivors of this great tradition.

By the beginning of the twentieth century the population of what is today's London Borough of Barnet had grown (and continued to grow) at a great rate. In 1801, for example, it had been a mere 8,000; by 1901 it was 76,000. To cater for their needs, hundreds of shops were opened around the turn of the century, many of them in purpose-built shopping parades. They includeed chain stores run by entrepreneurs such as Sainsbury and Boot, whose business empires survive to this day. Many were family-run businesses specialising in one type of goods, and whose customers came from nearby houses. Of particular interest were the so-called 'corner-shops' – rather like village stores – located at the end of housing terraces. They sold a wide variety of goods including foodstuffs, tobacco, sweets, newspapers and soft drinks. Such shops were centres for gossip and local news and were very much part of the social fabric. Their owners worked long hours for little reward and, especially in poorer areas, risked bad debts.

Wealthier customers or those living some distance from the shopping centre would have their goods delivered. Errand boys on bicycles and tricycles were a common sight as, later, were liveried vans. In some areas tradesmen such as fishmongers, butchers and greengrocers would call daily at the middle-class houses to display their products carefully arranged in a wicker basket. At larger houses (or those with pretensions to grandeur) the visit would be via the 'tradesman's entrance', with decisions taken by the housekeeper or cook.

Milk and bread were delivered daily although both products could also be obtained from local shops. Many housewives baked their own bread. Before the advent of glass bottles in the 1920s, milk was carried in churns on carts and dispensed into individual cans ranging in size from $\frac{1}{2}$ pint to 2 quarts. Butter and eggs were also sold and, at Christmas time, turkeys and chickens. The milkman made two rounds every day. His hours were very long for small wages and it is perhaps not too surprising that many of them 'fiddled' their customers – often in league with the housekeeper!

The years between the two world wars saw many changes in retailing. Even in the more sophisticated multiple grocery stores such as Sainsbury's, Tesco's, the Cooperative Society and

Home & Colonial, the customer waited at the counter to be served by the shop assistant. Goods were stored in bulk. Butter, for example, would be taken from a large block, pounded into a convenient shape and wrapped in wax-paper. Cheese was cut from a block by a wire while bacon and ham were cut from a shoulder or leg by a rotating slicer or sharp knife. Biscuits were sold loose, as were coffee beans, pulses and sugar – all of them weighed loose and packed into a paper bag. Payment was often a lengthy business, with the assistant recording and pricing all purchases on a piece of paper. In the more modern stores, money would be sent to a central cashier by a remarkable overhead wire conveyor or vacuum tube system. Queueing was an accepted part of life.

The post office, with its numerous main and sub-offices, has remained for many people an indispensable part of life. One of the main changes to be observed is that many are run today by Asian proprietors who combine the traditional services of the post office with those of retailing newspapers, magazines, confectionery and a host of other products. Here again, long hours and hard work have been essential to achieve success.

Self-service and the Supermarket

In the late 1950s the supermarket revolution reached Britain from the United States. The concept of 'serving yourself' with pre-packed, pre-weighed and already priced goods revolutionised shopping. The huge purchasing power of the supermarkets enabled them to offer goods at a low price, but this inevitably led to hundreds of smaller shops going out of business. Additionally, the supermarkets were able to offer car parking space and check-out counters which employed electronic calculators and bar codes to minimise mistakes and took credit cards in payment for goods. The growth in ownership of refrigerators and deep-freezers made weekly shopping trips possible for most households.

The supermarkets and the hypermarkets located outside towns continued to put pressure on the smaller shops. Their product range is continually being extended and now embraces goods such as flowers, plants, clothes, toys, photographic film, greetings cards, newspapers, books and petrol – goods that were previously sold by smaller specialist shops. More change is in the air with the advent of computer shopping.

Another great change has been the shopping mall. Brent Cross was one of the earliest and most successful of these enterprises and now enjoys unprecedented popularity, with customers coming from all parts of the UK. Similar schemes are planned for 'redundant' sites such as Friern Hospital.

The Ethnic Revolution

Barnet's large ethnic population has been responsible in part for the popularity and huge demand for ethnic food. Their family-run restaurants and shops have revolutionised eating habits with citizens now enjoying dishes (suitably modified to meet western tastes) from all over the world. Just as popular are take-away meals supplied principally by Chinese and Indian restaurants. Their menus even include that most traditional of British fare – fish and chips!

This studio model of a typical small Victorian/Edwardian grocer's shop gives a fascinating insight into shopping methods which still existed up to the early 1950s. The concept of pre-packaging and pricing had not yet arrived. Many goods were displayed in bulk with purchases put into paper bags and twists of paper. The service was slow and queuing frequent. Much less attention was paid to hygiene than today, with counters, shelves and sacks open to dust, dirt and flies. A shop cat to control vermin was not unusual! That said, such shops were inviting and enjoyable meeting places in which to exchange gossip and pleasantries. Part of the shopkeeper's skill was to know his customers by name and something of their background and problems. Many customers would expect delivery of their purchases to their home.

Around 1905 the demand for fresh milk and other dairy products for newly developed areas such as Hampstead Garden Suburb and Golders Green was met by small local dairy farms who delivered to the door. Each household at that time would have its own milk can filled from a churn although, later, bottles would become increasingly in demand. There were at least two deliveries a day, every day of the year.

Rose's ironmongery and oilstore in the High Road, Whetstone, *c.* 1910. The photograph shows the enormous range of products handled by such stores. Larger items such as dustbins would be displayed on the pavement. Part of their stock-in-trade was whale oil for lamps and bundles of firewood for kindling coal fires.

Baughen's was a well-known family business in Chipping Barnet. This photograph shows two of their shops in Church Passage in around 1900. It was not unusual for a family to run several shops of different kinds including, as here, a building and undertaking business which often went together. The Baughens also ran a tailoring business in Chipping Barnet which, among other things, was contracted by a church charity to supply winter overcoats for 'the deserving poor'.

Mr and Mrs Beaumont's shop, the Sailors' Home, in Whetstone's High Road, *c.* 1910. Such shops demanded long hours and the rewards were small. Regular customers came from nearby houses and could purchase a wide range of goods ranging from ham on-the-bone to soft drinks and soap flakes. Passing trade, such as Sunday cyclists, was also important. They were supplied with light refreshments including, in the summer months, home-made ice-cream.

Golders Green Road, 1920s. The box tricycle in the foreground was a popular method for delivering goods of every description. It was also famously used by Walls' Ice-cream whose slogan was 'Stop Me and Buy One'. The butcher's shop on the right, with its open frontage displaying carcases of meat, was a typical feature of those days. Fishmongers used similar shops.

Brent Street, Hendon, c. 1905. This was the main shopping centre for the area. The Smith & Son fascia shows that the tea-shop had formerly been used to sell pianos! The stationery shop next door housed a circulating library where books could be hired for a small charge. Such shops were made obsolete with the coming of public libraries.

Bolton's Stores, near the junction of Hammers Lane and the Ridgeway, Mill Hill, in the early years of the century. The store was also the local post office and the three telegraph boys with their bicycles are a reminder of the time when telephones were rare and urgent communication was through the very speedy and efficient telegram service run by the post office.

Many of today's sub-post offices, which provide an essential service to local residents, are run by Asian families. The service is frequently combined, as in this one in Sunny Gardens Parade, Hendon, with the sale of newspapers, tobacco, confectionery and groceries.

Many of the small dairy farms in the borough eventually sold out to the large combines such as United Dairies and the Express Dairy. The old handcarts were replaced by horse and cart with milkmen dressed in company livery. This photograph, taken in Friern Barnet Lane in the 1930s, shows Harry Broadbelt who originally owned Floyd's Dairy Farm in Friern Barnet Lane – the site of today's police station.

By the 1930s, and in some cases much earlier, the larger shops and chain stores began to pay attention to the style and appearance of their premises. This delightful wall-tile feature, one of a series of animals, came from Dewhurst's butcher's shop in North Finchley.

Jackson's coal wharf in Market Place, East Finchley, *c.* 1920. The Jacksons supplied coal and coke to the neighbourhood, some of it collected by the householders themselves in wheelbarrows and even old prams. Mr Jackson, who left much of the work to his wife (pictured here), was the first Labour councillor to be elected to Finchley Council.

During the Second World War goods of every description were in short supply, placing heavy burdens on both shopkeeper and customer. Window display was largely pointless and some shops, such as this one in High Road, Finchley, took the opportunity to use their windows for patriotic themes. The Wings for Victory campaign displayed here (March 1943) was a National Savings campaign in which, by purchasing stamps and savings certificates, it was possible to 'buy' a Spitfire and help to win the war. It was a triumph of propaganda and wishful thinking over common sense but it was all in a good cause!

Car boot sales, popular for many years in countries such as Australia, have mushroomed in Britain in recent years. This one, in East Barnet, shows that the original concept of a car-boot has grown into a van plus tables and display cases! The sales are extremely popular, with low prices making for quick sales. It is a matter of some regret that car boot sales are notorious outlets for stolen goods.

One of the greatest changes of the last half of the twentieth century has been the advent, and increasing popularity, of ethnic foods. Every High Street in the borough has its restaurants and take-aways supplying dishes originating from all parts of the world. Among the most popular are Chinese and Indian restaurants such as this one in High Street, Barnet, pictured in 1998.

Barnet Market, 1998. The market received its charter in 1199 and has been on its present site in St Alban's Road since 1851. Today, it is a stall market, in contrast with earlier days when livestock was sold – the last such auction took place in the 1950s. Currently, the future of the market is in some doubt.

The huge demand for computers and associated software has resulted in specialist computer stores, such as this one which opened in the Edgware Road in the 1990s. Although self-service is encouraged, specialist staff are on duty to help with customer queries and advice.

The Viking launderette, Bittacy Hill, 1999. The advent of the domestic washing-machine transformed for many people the drudgery and hard work of the traditional wash-day. A further development was the so-called launderette where large washing-machines and tumble-dryers can be hired to do a family-size weekly wash in an hour or so. Staff are also on hand to do the washing for an extra charge.

The Spires shopping centre in Chipping Barnet, 1998. Built on land previously occupied by a military barracks and a Methodist church, the centre is an attractive complex of smaller shops and a supermarket with an open area for seating and relaxation. An adjacent multi-storey car park connected with the centre is an added attraction for many shoppers.

Chapter Eight
Public Services

Marylebone Cemetery, East Finchley, 1998. This memorial to Sir Peter
Nicol Burnett (1816–1905) stands in St Marylebone cemetery, East
Finchley. The borough accommodates cemeteries for other parts of
North London, including St Marylebone and Islington. Apart from
parish churchyards, our borough has no specific burial ground of its
own. A feature of the last quarter of the century has been the opening
of burial grounds for non-Christian religious groups.

PUBLIC SERVICES

Until comparatively recently there was little provision of care for the sick and elderly. Those who could work and earn money survived; those who could not died unless they could get help. Susan Payne of Totteridge, aged sixty-five, for example, was 'looked after by Christian neighbours'. Churches or monasteries sometimes provided help and there were a few almshouses. The dissolution of the monasteries after 1536, the increasing movement of people from the country to the town and the general increase in population after the Black Death simply exacerbated the problem. From 1547 onwards a series of laws placed the responsibility for dealing with the poor on the local parish.

Local residents were required to hold office as Poor Law Guardians and were appointed annually. Meetings for the purpose were usually parish based and came to be called the vestry. Decisions taken at these vestry meetings were recorded by a clerk, the precursor of the modern town clerk. The posts to be filled included the surveyor of the highways, who dealt with raising money and organising labour for roads; the overseer of the poor, who was responsible for collecting and distributing poor relief; an ale-taster (not the sinecure it might be imagined); and sometimes, though not always, the parish constable. The vestry had the power to levy a rate on property to meet its expenses.

The Welfare of the Poor

The system of poor relief was cumbersome and expensive and was changed by the Poor Law Act of 1834, which grouped parishes into Unions. Most local parishes had previously operated their own local poor house. These were closed when the Union house was opened. In the Union house paupers were required to work for their keep, hence the term workhouse. Hadley workhouse had a treadmill in 1821.

The Barnet Union Workhouse for Barnet, Finchley, Hadley, etc., was built in Wellhouse Lane in 1835. It had separate wards for men, women and children, and an infirmary. Admittance was unpopular because families were split up. Hendon Union Workhouse catered for Hendon, Edgware and a large area towards Willesden.

The Union houses each had an infirmary, with a doctor on hand, paid for out of the poor rates. It was from these small beginnings that our local hospitals developed.

Public Health

At the end of Queen Victoria's reign there was little in the district that we would recognise as a hospital. The rich went to private sanatoria. The poor went to the workhouse. Those in between had to pay for medical treatment. Various local charities began building small cottage hospitals. Middlesex County Council also began building such hospitals. The role of the local authorities in developing public health is often overlooked.

The National Health Service, which was established with wide support in 1942, introduced the idea of medical care that is free at the point of delivery. This was not just to revolutionise the treatment of illness, but also, coupled with improvements in diet and medical knowledge, to increase life expectancy. The Second World War hastened the development of life-saving drugs, in particular penicillin, while the last years of the century saw the rapid growth in medical technology, keyhole surgery and the use of computers. By the end of the twentieth century, people of seventy-five did not consider themselves to be old.

An unusual growth industry in the district was the creation of large municipal burial grounds in places like Hendon, Finchley and Brunswick Park to supplement overused parish churchyards. The demand for cremation also led to the construction of the Golders Green and other crematoria.

Rubbish Disposal

Litter and rubbish collection and sewage disposal were gradually taken over by local boards. Main drains were dug progressively after 1860, largely as a result of the Sanitary Act of 1866, though earth closets were still in use as late as 1895. Sewage farms were built at the foot of Barnet Hill, in East Barnet valley, along Strawberry Vale in Finchley and in other suitable low-lying places. Piped water mains were installed at about the same time.

A high level sewer serving Barnet, Finchley and Friern Barnet and running down the Dollis Valley and near the North Circular Road leading to Pickets Lock in Enfield, was built by Middlesex County Council in 1937. There is a subsidiary sewer down East Barnet Valley. The Hendon side of the borough is served by the Mogden Lane site in Isleworth; also built in the 1930s, it is capable of dealing with 198 million gallons a day. In April 1997 Thames Water assumed responsibility for sewerage in the borough.

Domestic and industrial waste and rubbish were originally buried in land-fill sites; indeed many school playing fields are laid out on the rubbish tips of the first half of the century. Later years brought increased environmental awareness and by 1999 about 6 per cent of the total 110,000 tonnes of rubbish was being recycled. Much of the remainder goes to land-fill sites outside the borough.

Local Councils

By about 1880 matters were so complicated that a complete reorganisation of local government was needed. The result was the 1894 Act which set up a number of county and local councils. Barnet, East Barnet, Hendon, Friern Barnet and Finchley, for example, all became Urban or Rural Districts. As a result of the Local Government Act of 1963, the various local authorities combined in April 1965 to form the London Borough of Barnet.

Heat and Light

The need for heat and light was also met in the late Victorian period. The Colney Hatch Gas Company at New Southgate (1858), the North Middlesex Gas Company (1862) at Mill Hill, supplying Hendon, Mill Hill and Finchley, and the Barnet District Gas and Water Company are examples. The various local companies were combined to form the Gas Board in 1948 and were privatised and separated again some fifty years later.

Finchley Corporation had its own electricity supply works in Squires Lane from 1900, substantially enlarged in 1903. Most of the district was served by the North Metropolitan Electricity Company until control passed to the Eastern Electricity Board around 1955. This, too, was privatised in the late 1980s.

Police

The duties of the parish constable, sometimes aided by a watchman, became ever more demanding as the population increased and legislation became more complex. The district was included in the Metropolitan Police area by 1840, prior to which the Bow Street horse patrol had covered the main roads.

Colney Hatch Hospital, 1850. Colney Hatch Asylum for the Lunatic Poor was opened by Prince Albert. Most of the money, however, came from the public purse. Made of some ten million bricks dug locally and with about 6 miles of corridors and wards, it was one of the largest buildings in Europe. From the first it was run on the principles of kindness, and the use of restraint was forbidden. In the hospital's first years, between 40 per cent and 60 per cent of patients recovered and were discharged within six months. At the other end of the scale, though, 19 per cent died. Following the introduction of Care in the Community, the hospital was closed and the land sold in 1993 to make way for housing and a large retail park. The splendid Victorian façade has, however, been preserved.

Celebrating the Coronation of King Edward VII at Barnet Workhouse, 1902. Barnet Workhouse was opened in 1835. It had separate wards for men, women and children and included an infirmary (now the Rosemary unit). The infirmary became the basis of Barnet Hospital. The site was exensively developed in 1916, with operating theatres and six wards opened to deal with war casualties, when it was renamed Wellhouse Hospital. Dr H. Roland Segar, a notable medical pioneer, was Medical Superintendent here from 1925 until 1952. New buildings for the state of the art Wellhouse NHS Trust Hospital opened in April 1997.

Bomb damage at Colindale Hospital, 1941. The foundation stone was laid on 6 June 1898. The buildings were designed as a County Hospital for the Sick Poor and were as far out into the 'healthy countryside' as possible. In 1920 the hospital was reclassified for use by advanced TB patients. It was taken over by the LCC in 1930. The hospital was damaged by a landmine in the winter of 1940/41 and by a flying bomb in 1944.

Edgware General Hospital, 1936. In 1997 this hospital was the subject of a huge campaign to prevent its closure. It was built as Redhill Hospital by the Hendon Board of Guardians in 1927. Since then it has been owned in turn by Middlesex County Council, the National Health Service and the Wellhouse NHS Trust. There were extensions in 1938 featuring typical 1930s glass and steel structures. New theatres and a sterile store were added in 1964 and 1966.

Hendon Town Hall, *c.* 1903. The town hall was designed by T.H. Watson. It was opened in 1901 and enlarged in 1934. Following the creation of the London Borough of Barnet in 1963, it now houses the council chamber, the town clerk's department and various finance offices. By April 1999 the total expenditure of the Borough was said to be £254,295,010.

Barnet House, Whetstone, 1998. This building dominates the skyline at Whetstone crossroads. It is used by the various departments of Barnet Council which are concerned with the environment.

North Finchley Library, 1936. Finchley public library was opened in 1935. The *Finchley Press* of the day published a complaint from a local shopkeeper that it was impossible for his staff to use the library because it closed at 8 in the evening before his staff had finished work. By the end of the century, libraries were offering computers on loan as well as video-tapes and compact disks.

The Borough Archives, 1997. The Archives and Local Studies Department of the Barnet Libraries is housed in Egerton Gardens, Hendon. It holds a comprehensive collection of local historical and geographic material and is staffed by experts. It is visited not just by local school parties and residents but by researchers from all over the country.

Building the sewers under Finchley, *c.* 1920. In 1935 the *Finchley Press* reported 'A cloudburst broke on Thursday evening when no less than three million tons of rain fell on an area measuring four miles by two miles'. Pymmes Brook in East Barnet burst its banks, causing widespread flooding in Crescent Road.

Loading a dust cart, Hendon, 1920. Controlled tipping into land-fill sites created the foundations for many of the borough's playing fields. By the end of the century 'Green' thinking had become prevalent and there were attempts to recycle waste materials; for example, about 1.8 million newspapers are recycled every week. In 1999 refuse disposal in the borough was costing nearly ten million pounds a year.

The Finchley Corporation Electricity Works, Squires Lane, *c.* 1920. The electricity works of the former Finchley Council were opened in Squires Lane around 1899. The large lake intended to supply cooling water was very attractive to mosquitos and so in 1937 the lake was stocked with goldfish which grew very large.

New Barnet gasometer, 1998. The New Barnet Gas Company built its works next to the railway to provide easy access for the coal waggons, as did the others at Mill Hill and Colney Hatch. The use of gas for street lighting was limited in 1871 by the proviso that the lamps were not to be lit on moonlight nights. The use of gas for domestic purposes in Victorian times was a great improvement on oil lighting and coal.

Barnet police station, c. 1890. At that time Barnet was not part of the Metropolitan Police District. The local police were paid less than their colleagues in the rest of the borough which was included in the Met. Several police stations were closed during the 1990s and the opening hours of others were reduced. Many regret the passing of the 'bobby on the beat'. In 1999 there are six stations covering the borough at a cost of about ten million pounds a year.

Finchley fire brigade, *c.* 1920. This station was closed and replaced by a new station on the North Circular Road in 1936. A new station in Barnet was opened in 1993. The number of fire engines stationed in the district was cut in 1998/9 in spite of widespread public protest. In that year the Fire Service cost the average household £27.57 a year.

Friern Barnet ambulance station, 1998. Modern communications techniques and advances in paramedic training have led to the centralisation of ambulances and the introduction of rapid response teams. Modern ambulances carry a comprehensive set of equipment.

Barnet Carnival, *c.* 1900. Although much of the funding for public services has come from the public purse, there have been many efforts to raise money privately. Carnivals were very popular in the first seventy-five years of the century. This is Syd Laidlaw on his decorated tricycle, raising money for Victoria Cottage Hospital.

The Wright Kingsford Children's Home, Finchley, *c.* 1935. The home was founded in 1898 by Miss Blanche Wright and Miss Kingsford for ten babies at Granville Road, Finchley. By the time this picture was taken there were about 128 children in residence at a cost of about £5,000 a year. Financial supporters included the Shaftesbury Society, local schools, businesses and cinemas. It held a very popular annual summer fête. The home was declared no longer fit for children in 1945 and was demolished shortly afterwards. By the end of the century orphanages such as this had been closed in favour of smaller units.

A NEW ARTERIAL ROAD.

A unique piece of road engineering is now being carried out at New Southgate where the North Circular-road is to link up Bowes Park and Finchley. In order to do this, the new section has to be carried under the L.N.E.R. main line. Meanwhile, rail traffic at this spot is slowed down to four

The North Circular Road, 1928. Around 1929 the North Circular Road at Friern Barnet was extended under the railway to link up with Bowes Road. The road was further widened in a cutting under Colney Hatch Lane in 1975, with additional improvements at East Finchley in 1996.

Edgware Register Office, 1998. The recording of births, marriages and deaths was the responsibility of the parish until 1838. One of the great changes of this century has been the amount of information that is now held on ordinary citizens, not just by the government but also by commercial organisations.

Hendon postman's office, *c.* 1920. By 1999 there were fourteen delivery offices covering the borough. In 1999 Hendon delivery office had fifty-six staff using five vehicles and dealt with about 250,000 items in an average week, rising to a million a week at Christmas.

Brunswick Park Health Centre, 1998. Centres such as this provide accommodation not just for doctors but also for a whole range of related services like specialist clinics and often a pharmacy. There was controversy over this particular building in 1998 when it was threatened with closure.

Chapter Nine
The Borough at War

The Evacuation from Dunkirk, 1940. French soldiers (notice the helmets) arrived at New Southgate station on 1 June 1940 following the evacuation from Dunkirk. Most of them were accommodated in the Great Hall at Alexandra Palace before being dispersed to military camps across the country.

THE BOROUGH AT WAR

A combination of ancient usage dating back to Anglo-Saxon times and statute laws passed since that time made all able-bodied men aged between sixteen and sixty liable to perform military duties within their own counties. The Statute of Winchester (1285) required men to equip themselves with specific arms and armour according to their income. There were archery butts at the junction of Friern Barnet Lane and the Whetstone High Road (where the Esso garage now stands), where local citizens were required to practise archery.

The first part-time soldiers about whom there is any good record is the Herts. Yeomanry. The Southern Independent troop was formed at Barnet in 1794. They wore a blue uniform with red facings. The South Mimms and Hadley Volunteers – consisting of twenty men – were commanded by the Hon. George Byng.

Barnet Barracks were built around 1859 (on what is now the site of the Spires shopping centre) and were occupied by regular troops including (in 1911) the 7th Battalion Middlesex Regiment. During the Second World War the barracks were occupied by Royal Army Pay Corps staff who sent out the cheques to pay the army's bills. Indeed it could be argued that the war was won from Barnet.

The Twentieth Century

Inglis Barracks were built on spare land at the top of Bittacy Hill, Mill Hill, and opened in April 1905. They were the depot of the Middlesex Regiment. In 1940 a REME Command workshop was built lower down the hill. This is now used as a council road depot. During the period of National Service, the barracks were used as a basic training centre.

The Middlesex Regiment was amalgamated with others to form the London Brigade and moved away in January 1961. The site was then used as a postal and courier depot. The depot was attacked by the IRA in August 1988 when L/Cpl Michael Robins was killed.

The numerous married quarters which had been built were not all needed and the Notting Hill Housing Trust bought eleven four-bedroom houses and eighty-four flats to provide 'affordable' houses for rent.

The First World War (1914–18)

The local unit, the Middlesex Regiment, based at Mill Hill barracks, formed part of the British Expeditionary Force that sailed for France between 12 and 16 August 1914. The 4th battalion was one of the first units to engage the Germans, at Mons on 23/24 August 1914, where they were covering the bridge at Obourg. Casualties were heavy, and by the evening of 24 August only 275 men out of 1,000 were present at roll call.

By 1916 the professional army of 1914 had been wiped out and replaced by Kitchener's army of volunteers. Fifteen battalions of the Middlesex regiment fought during the battle of the Somme in 1916 when casualty lists made grim reading. In all, there were some 56,000 casualties on the first morning of the battle – that is, roughly equal to the population of Finchley. The second battalion of the Middlesex Regiment lost 22 out of 23 officers and 600 out of 650 other ranks in Mash Valley attacking towards Ovillers. In all, there were forty-six line battalions of the Middlesex Regiment plus works units.

The regiment may possibly have fired the last shot of the war. When the Armistice took effect at 11 a.m. on 11 November 1918, the 2nd battalion was about 4 miles from Mons. It was here that the firing ceased.

Number 2 company of the Hertfordshire Volunteer Regiment was formed at Barnet in 1916. By 1917 the total strength of the regiment was 2,500 and two volunteer motor field ambulance units were formed.

Casualties from the battlefields made huge demands on local resources; for example, Manor House Hospital was built, Barnet Hospital was extended in 1916, wards at Colney Hatch were used to treat the wounded and the hall at Hampstead Garden Suburb was commandeered. Many local halls and buildings were taken over to house casualties.

The 1930s

The theory that 'the bomber will always get through' dominated military thinking in the 1930s. Nevertheless, the defence of London in the form of a ring of fighter aerodromes, anti-aircraft guns and searchlights was planned. In 1936 there was a great recruitment drive when units of the Territorial Army were formed. Most of the local units were Royal Engineers, part of 61 AA Brigade, working searchlights. Nos 332 and 333 companies were formed at Camden Town and included Highgate, Edgware and Hampstead; 334 at Barnet and 335 at Tottenham included New Southgate and Finchley, though there was no rigidity and men attended whichever drill hall was the most convenient.

By 1935 it was increasingly obvious that war was coming again and preparations should begin. One response to this was the idea of Civil Defence. Recruitment began in earnest in 1937 after government money was made available. Some permanent staff were appointed, together with a core of instructors. Staffing levels were worked out and the training of appropriate personnel began.

The Second World War (1939–45)

In 1939 young men were conscripted into existing military, naval and air force units. Seven battalions were formed for the Middlesex Regiment, who served in every theatre of operations. On the whole, however, the relationship between districts and local units was less formal than in the First World War and personnel were sent wherever they were needed. To some extent this was remedied when warships were 'adopted' by various localities. By 1941 young women, too, were being conscripted into the armed forces, or to work in factories and on the land.

The Home Guard

After the retreat from France in May 1940 a German invasion was expected at any moment. Civilian volunteers were recruited among older men and those in exempted occupations, to fight if necessary. At first they had no uniforms, only armbands. Weapons, too, were in short supply. Gradually things improved and the Home Guard made a valuable contribution to the war, not least by relieving regular troops from static guard duties.

The local units were 23 Battalion Middlesex Regiment (Home Guard), recruiting mostly from Mill Hill and Edgware, with a rifle range at Scratch Wood; 24 Battalion drawn from East and Friern Barnet, North Finchley, Totteridge and Hendon; and 46 County of London Battalion formed from London Transport staff including Finchley and Hendon bus garages. The Standard Factory at East Barnet was defended by the AA Bofors guns of A Troop 29 Middlesex Battalion.

Troops of the 3rd (Volunteer) Battalion Hertfordshire Regiment at Barnet Barracks in 1918. These part-time soldiers were for home defence only and also had civilian jobs. The unit was disbanded in November 1918 and this photograph was probably taken on that occasion. The corporal on the left of the front row is 'Curly' Hayes, later caretaker at Queen Elizabeth's School for Boys. Sergeant Hyde is on the extreme right with the swagger stick.

The regimental band of the Middlesex Regiment at Inglis Barracks, Mill Hill, c. 1924. Most bandsmen could play both a wind and a stringed instrument. The men were trained in First Aid and in wartime acted as stretcher-bearers.

Troops from 334 Company Royal Engineers at Barnet Drill Hall, 1938. They were mobilised in 1938 just before Neville Chamberlain and Hitler signed the Munich agreement promising 'Peace in our time'. There was insufficient military transport and civilian buses were commandeered. Major Fellowes (centre) and Captain Tasker (right) are receiving a report from Lieutenant Lancaster.

Brickhouse Farm, Hunsden, September 1939. Men of 334 Company manned searchlights as part of London's defensive ring. On this site the men were able to use the nearby farm for a weekly bath. On 8 September 1940 the men were warned, 'Invasion imminent. Probably within 12 hours. Each man will go into the woods and cut himself a stout cudgel.'

These 4.5-inch heavy anti-aircraft guns were based at Sweet's Nursery, Whetstone, in 1940. The site was known by the codename Glasshouses. There were other gun sites at Mill Hill and Hadley and a Bofors gun site at the Standard Factory in Whetstone. The units serving the guns were rotated.

The Finchley Home Guard Company included a platoon stationed at the electricity works in Squires Lane. The Home Guard (originally called the Local Defence Volunteers) was formed in the summer of 1940, initially to repel an expected invasion. They eventually became a highly trained and skilful body of men.

The interior of post number one, District A, East Barnet Civil Defence Region, on Hadley Green. The lynch-pin of the Civil Defence system was the air raid warden who acted as the eyes and ears for the rest of the system. Swift and accurate reporting was essential.

Erecting Anderson shelters at North Finchley, 1939. These shelters were made of corrugated steel sheets and were sunk about 3 ft into the ground. They would protect against splinters and flying debris but could not withstand a direct hit from a bomb. They were named after their inventor, Dr David A. Anderson, a Home Office scientist, and not after Sir John Anderson as is popularly supposed.

War production, 1916. The McCurd lorry factory was opened in the High Road, North Finchley, in 1916. It was quickly enlarged and made ammunition as well. Large numbers of women were recruited to replace men working on the machines.

War production, 1940. The Standard factory in New Southgate was opened in 1922. At its peak during the Second World War it employed some 14,000 people making highly complicated electronic equipment, including radar. In 1944 the telephone apparatus for General Eisenhower's headquarters was made here. Owned in 1999 by Nortel, the factory still produces state-of-the-art electronics.

Friern Barnet Town Hall, 1941. The campaign to get the population to save instead of spend was one of the most successful of the war years. People were encouraged to believe that their savings certificates would actually buy a Spitfire or other weapons.

HMS *Ursa* was 'adopted' by the Borough of Hendon. She was an Ulster class destroyer of 1,710 tons, launched in March 1943, with a crew of about 190. Her armament included four 4.5-inch guns, smaller weapons and depth-charges. Her dual three-drum boilers could drive her engines to produce 34 knots. Ships of this type cost about £350,000 each to build.

The Women's Voluntary Service, 1941. The WVS was formed in 1938 and quickly proved to be a most valuable resource. The women helped in any emergency situation where welfare or comfort was needed, particularly after bombing raids.

VE Day street party, May 1945. The end of the war in Europe on 8 May 1945 was marked by widespread celebrations, including street parties. Food was rationed but mums managed to provide enough butter and sugar to produce cakes, jellies and other goodies which the children had not tasted since 1939.

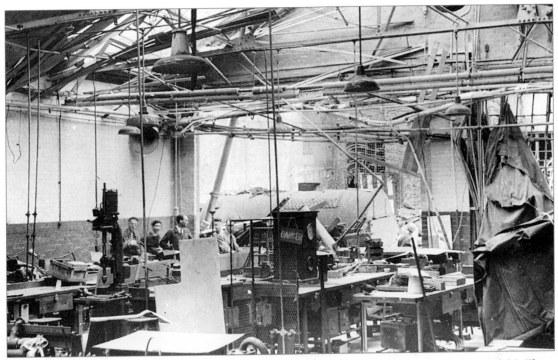

Bomb damage, East Barnet, 1944. The Standard factory was hit by a flying bomb on 23 August 1944. There was extensive damage and 33 people were killed, 212 seriously wounded and 218 slightly wounded.

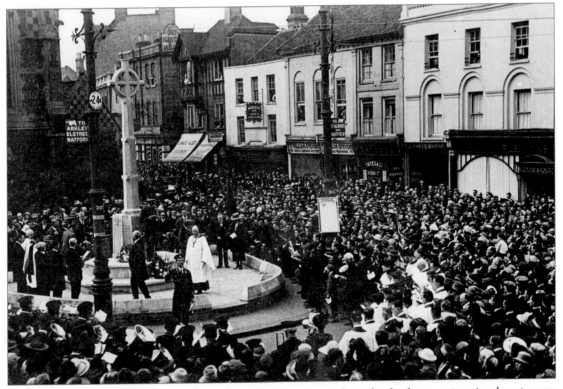

Barnet war memorial, 1922. After the First World War memorials to the dead were set up in almost every parish and in many schools and factories as well. General Byng of Vimy unveiled the Barnet war memorial. In 1936 it was deemed to be an obstruction to traffic and was moved into the nearby churchyard.

BOROUGH OF HENDON

St. Michael's British Restaurant

(St. Michael's Church Hall,
The Riding, Golders Green, N.W.11)

OPEN FOR PUBLIC USE

from

MONDAY, JULY 13th, 1942

MID-DAY MEALS SERVED

from

12 noon to 2 p.m. each week-day

SCALE OF PRICES

Soup - - - -	2d.
Entrée and two Vegetables -	10d.
plus one piece of bread	
Milk Pudding - - -	2d.
Steamed Pudding plus one sauce -	3d.
Cup of Tea - - -	1d.
Cup of Coffee - - -	2d.

Customers who bring their own crockery may take meals home

Printed by WARDEN & CO. LTD., 71, Church Road, Hendon, N.W.4.

Hendon British Restaurant, 1942. The need to release women to work in factories led to the introduction of school dinners and the British Restaurant, where balanced and mainly vegetarian meals were available cheaply. Not surprisingly, the nation's health was actually better during the war.

In order to help to relieve the food shortages caused by the German U-boat blockade, food scraps known as pig wash were collected by the pig cart and recycled. This is possibly a publicity photograph, because the label specifically warns against putting rhubarb leaves into the bin.

Do you remember when the headlines said—

"No potatoes for this Sunday's joint"

While thousands of housewives enjoyed another little grumble, the wiser families who had dug for victory enjoyed their Sunday joint with all the potatoes and other vegetables they wanted.   Learn from experience.   To be sure of the family's vegetables, you must grow them yourselves—women and older children as well as men.   If you haven't a garden, ask your Local Council for an allotment.   Start to

DIG FOR VICTORY NOW!

POST THIS COUPON NOW (Unsealed envelope, 1d. stamp)

TO MINISTRY OF AGRICULTURE, HOTEL LINDUM, ST. ANNES-ON-SEA, LANCS.
Please send me copies of free pictorial leaflets, "How to Dig" and "How to Crop"

NAME ....

ADDRESS ....

B.99

ISSUED   BY   THE   MINISTRY   OF   AGRICULTURE

EAST BARNET URBAN DISTRICT COUNCIL.

SALVAGE OF WASTE MATERIALS

DO NOT WASTE YOUR PAPER

The Council will collect all your waste paper including newspaper, cardboard, magazines, old books, etc.

Please keep your paper and place it on your dust bin or give it to the dustman when he calls each week.

RAW MATERIAL IS WAR MATERIAL

[P.T.O.

The need to maximise shipping space for war materials led to salvage drives intended to recycle materials. These 1942 advertisements are examples of the kind of publicity prevalent at the time.

FRIERN BARNET
HOLIDAYS AT HOME

THE WEEK'S PROGRAMME

SUNDAY, AUGUST 1st
United Churches Programme.
Friary Park. Open Air Service.
8.30 p.m.

MONDAY, AUGUST 2nd
FETE AND PROCESSION
Friary Park. 2 p.m.
Open Air Dancing.
Side Shows. Tug-of-War, etc.
Southgate British Legion Band
and Sea Cadets Band will play
in procession. Southgate British
Legion Band at night.

TUESDAY, AUGUST 3rd
Baby Show. Preliminary Judging.
Friary Park. 3 to 5 p.m.
Mobile Cinema.
War Savings Van. Friary Park.
6 to 9 p.m.
Open Air Dancing.
N.F.S. Orchestra.
Friary Park. 7 p.m.

WEDNESDAY, AUGUST 4th
Police Band. Friary Park.
7.30 p.m., Open Air Dancing.

THURSDAY, AUGUST 5th
Will Gardner's War Time Follies.
Friary Park. 7.30 p.m.
Tickets 2/- and 1/-.

FRIDAY, AUGUST 6th
Mobile Cinema.
War Savings Van. Friary Park.
3 to 5 p.m.
Whist and Bridge Drives.
Town Hall. Tickets 2/-. 7 p.m.
Open Air Dancing. Friary Park.
N.F.S. Orchestra. 7.30 p.m.

SATURDAY, AUGUST 7th
CYCLE RACING, N.C.U. Rules)
LONDON CENTRE.
Halliwick Recreation Ground.
5.30 p.m.
A.R.P. Demonstration Van.
Town Hall Forecourt. 3 p.m.
Summer Dance.
British Restaurant. N.F.S. Band.
Tickets 2/6. 7.30 to 10.30 p.m.

Full particulars from F. T. TURNER, (Hon. Gen. Sec.), Town Hall, N.11.

Finchley Joint Entertainment Committee

FINCHLEY'S "HOLIDAY AT HOME" PROGRAMME

SUNDAY, AUGUST 1st
Return Visit of
DAVY JONES AND HIS NAUTICAL ORCHESTRA
AVENUE HOUSE GROUNDS, 7.30 P.M.
BANK HOLIDAY MONDAY, August 2nd
DEE ONE PLAYERS REVUE—"HELLO FINCHLEY"
AVENUE HOUSE GROUNDS—Matinee 3 p.m., Evening 7.30 p.m.
(If wet, ST. LUKE'S HALL, Mountfield Road, N.3)
OPEN AIR DANCE (H.M. Middlesex Regiment Dance Band)
STANLEY ROAD PLAYING FIELDS, 7.30 P.M.

Newspaper advertisement, 1942. There were several reasons for taking holidays at home. Seaside hotels were used for war purposes. Fuel for trains was scarce. The slogan 'Is your journey really necessary?' was used. Many mothers were recruited for war work and the need to entertain their children and the general need to keep morale high during the war led not only to public entertainments but to the creation of many local concert parties or dramatic groups.

Chapter Ten
The Environment

Although most of the borough's large Georgian, Victorian and Edwardian houses have long since disappeared and their gardens sold to make way for housing estates, reminders of their former glory can still be found. Joseph Baxendale's property on the corner of Totteridge Lane and High Road, Whetstone, is a good example. Although the house has been demolished, part of Baxendale's splendid lake, dotted with small islands, still survives. In addition to fish, it is home to a variety of waterfowl, marginal plants, flowers and trees. The residents of the Baxendale retirement home, which can be seen at the back of this 1998 photograph, look out on this pleasant view.

THE ENVIRONMENT

Flora and Fauna

It is difficult now to believe that at one time most of today's borough was covered in forest, with trees such as oak, ash, elm and hornbeam supporting a wide variety of wildlife. Over the centuries, the forest was cut down to make clearings for hamlets and fields and to provide London with timber for fuel and building.

The area was one of considerable natural beauty and it was a popular venue for Londoners keen to get away from the smoke and grime of the city. The coming of the railways around the middle of the nineteenth century, however, resulted in big increases in population and a subsequent demand locally for land for houses, roads, public buildings and the like. Thus began the pressure on locations such as meadowland, hedgerows, ponds and streams – the habitats of plants and animals.

In 1997 the London Ecology Unit published their Handbook 28: *Nature Conservation in Barnet*, which covers in great detail the plants, animals and habitats of no fewer than sixty-seven sites in today's borough. No comparable surveys exist for the beginning of the twentieth century although much was observed and recorded on specific topics, particularly birds and wild flowers. Direct comparisons are therefore difficult but, contrary to popular belief, it has not all been loss. Nature's remarkable adaptability plus imaginative laws such as the Town & Country Planning Act of 1947 have enabled many species to survive, and some have even prospered.

Homes and Gardens

The era of the great Victorian and Edwardian gardens, run by a large staff of full-time gardeners, has long since passed. They have been more than replaced (in wildlife terms) by a host of small suburban gardens lovingly tended by their owners who not only grow a remarkable range of flowers and shrubs but encourage birds to visit and breed in their gardens. Just as important are the small ponds that act as breeding places for frogs, newts and toads. Birdwatching has become a popular hobby and there is far less trapping and shooting than in earlier years. Foxes, too, are increasing in number. Their earths are often to be found beneath garden sheds and other outbuildings.

The coming of radio and television, with their excellent wildlife and nature programmes, has led to a growing understanding and appreciation of wildlife. Gardening, too, has benefited from such programmes and it is encouraging that places such as College Farm, the Barnet Countryside Centre and most schools now show an interest in natural history subjects.

The Green Corridors

The decrease in farmland combined with more intensive arable farming methods has badly affected small mammals and birds such as the tree sparrow which rely upon seeds, but the so-called green corridors formed by the railway embankments and motorways that criss-cross the borough have both stimulated the growth of many wild flowers and encouraged various birds such as kestrels and carrion crows that feed off the carcases of animals killed by traffic.

The many parks and open spaces managed by Barnet Council are also part of the green corridor. Although less well managed than in previous years, such places remain a sanctuary for flora and fauna. Some, such as Sunnyhill Park in Hendon, offer an interesting contrast between formal parkland, which is regularly mowed to provide sports pitches, and areas of untouched meadowland that provide an excellent habitat for a range of wild flowers, insects, birds, reptiles such as slow worms, and the slugs and snails upon which they feed. Other locations such as Avenue House, Finchley, contain outstanding collections of trees. Golf courses, cemeteries and allotments also play their part. A recent survey at the South Herts Golf Club off Totteridge Lane, for example, revealed hundreds of wild flowers including rose bay willow herb, enchanter's nightshade, mugwort and scarlet pimpernel. About 300 species of insects live on the willow trees and around 400 on the oaks – all of them a part of the food chain.

Waterways

The borough's most important stretch of water is probably Brent Reservoir (formerly Welsh Harp). Constructed in 1835, its 126 acres of water has attracted a wide variety of ducks and waterfowl throughout the century. In earlier times they were hunted, but today they are encouraged to breed by the erection of floating rafts and by allowing marginal vegetation to be established on parts of the shoreline. A particularly shameful episode from the past was the hunting of the great crested grebe almost to extinction merely to provide feathers for decorating hats. Happily, today it can be seen in some numbers.

Although the borough has no navigable river, its numerous brooks and streams are home to a variety of birds (including the kingfisher) and aquatic vegetation. The three-spined stickleback seems able to survive the pollution present in most of the streams. The disappearance of many farm ponds, dew ponds, lakes and the like has resulted in a serious decrease in the variety and number of amphibians such as newts, frogs and toads. Domestic ponds, as we have seen, offer some alternative but losses have been severe. Among the surviving ponds, Totteridge Long Pond is of particular interest because it is used by anglers and is kept stocked with fish such as carp. This encourages herons while coot and mallard breed on the pond. Dragonflies are often to be seen.

A near neighbour of the Long Pond is Darland's Nature Reserve with its artificial lake. This is an example of an area once privately owned but is today owned by Barnet Council and managed by a Wildlife Trust which encourages visitors throughout the year. Because of lack of resources, the lake is silted up, with bullrushes in the shallow water and willow and alder trees growing on the firmer ground. A variety of waterfowl can be seen and the area supports numerous birds including sparrowhawks, siskins, blackcaps and woodpeckers. No fewer than 120 species of fungi have been recorded and eighteen species of mammal including weasels and stoats. Bats, grass snakes and slow worms are also to be seen.

It took teams of gardeners to manage the large Victorian gardens such as this one at New Lodge, at the junction of Church Road and Brent Street, Hendon. There was great competition in local flower shows and it was an era when many new species of flowers, trees and plants were introduced into Britain for the first time. Complementing these innovations were greenhouses and conservatories growing exotic fruits and flowers.

Hadley Woods is the borough's largest example of a fully matured wood. It was originally part of the ancient Enfield Chase and is famous for its rare wild flowers and fungi. It has been a venue for pleasant walks throughout the century.

Allotments date back to the seventeenth and eighteenth centuries and the borough has a legal obligation to provide the necessary land. Today, 250 acres are set aside for this popular pastime and there are around four thousand plots located in various parts of the borough. Day-to-day management is often in the hands of the tenants themselves. This 1999 photograph was taken on the Archfields allotment site in Hendon.

The Welsh Harp reservoir is home to a wide variety of ducks and waterfowl. This 1998 photograph shows some of the floating rafts which provide additional nesting sites for the birds. A cormorant can be seen on the larger of the rafts.

South Herts Golf Club, Totteridge Lane, 1998. Careful management has ensured that the course is a haven for numerous species of birds, with bird boxes located in many of the trees, while special care is taken to preserve and protect the many species of trees and wild flowers.

This photograph of Sunnyhill Park, Hendon, illustrates how the borough has set aside parts of the park to remain wild, thus preserving the habitat of many wild flowers, insects and small mammals. Special efforts have been made to encourage the breeding of slow worms and grass snakes.

Decades

In this final section of the book, we present our selection of ten photographs, one for each decade of the century, which highlight some of the major events and changes that occurred in the London Borough of Barnet. We do not doubt that some readers will have different views about what was important in those years: we should be pleased to hear them.

1900–1909

The introduction of the electric tram to many parts of the borough from 1904 provided a cheap, frequent and reliable public transport service. In an era when work was scarce, manual and clerical workers could commute daily or look for work in other parts of London. Apart from local journeys, the trams connected with underground stations such as Golders Green with their service to London's City and the West End.

1910–1919

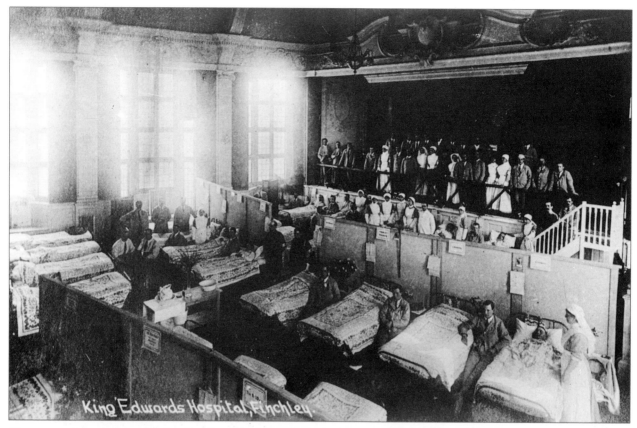

King Edwards Hospital, Finchley.

The numerous war memorials in all parts of the borough are testimony to the appalling casualties of the First World War. Problems arose with the huge number of wounded returning from the front, who overwhelmed the local hospitals. Temporary hospitals, such as this one in King Edward's Hall, Regents Park Road, Finchley, were set up to cope with the overflow. Many public buildings such as Finchley's Avenue House, the Clubhouse on Willifield Green, Hampstead Garden Suburb and even the Spalding Hall in Hendon were used for the same purpose. It was to be many years before the horrors of the war disappeared from public consciousness.

1920–1929

This was the decade of major expansion in the borough. There was a massive increase in population from 150,000 at the beginning of the decade to over 230,000 at its end. To meet their needs, new housing estates were built both for sale and rent; roads (including important trunk roads) were completed; new schools were built and existing ones expanded – all of this and more against a background of severe economic depression. This photograph, taken in Trinity Avenue, East Finchley in 1929, is a typical scene from those times. There was little machinery to do the hard work. Mortar was mixed by hand and carried in wooden wheelbarrows; bricks were carried in hods on the shoulders of the building labourer; building materials were delivered by horse and cart and manually off-loaded; and scaffolding poles were wooden and tied with wire bonds. Another typical sight was the nightwatchman's hut with its brazier of glowing coals in colder weather.

1930–1939

As the economy improved after the slumps of the earlier decade, more money became available to spend on leisure and entertainment. The cinema was then in its heyday and weekly visits to the local cinema were popular among all social classes. New cinemas were built, many of them with exotic decorative themes that encouraged feelings of escapism and glamour. This photograph shows the opening of the Odeon, Barnet, in 1935.

1940–1949

In little more than twenty years after the holocaust of the First World War, the Second broke out and the civilian populations, once again, became the target of enemy bombers. One of the worst local incidents occurred in February 1941 when a 1000kg bomb devastated Hendon's Ramsey, Ravenstone, York and Argyle Roads. Eighty people were killed and forty houses totally destroyed.

1950–1959

This decade, among other things, heralded what was called at the time the new Elizabethan Age. The shortages of wartime were still being overcome but, with the Festival of Britain in 1951, the outlook seemed much brighter. Dominating the decade was the coronation of Queen Elizabeth II. Seen here is the proclamation of the new sovereign on 2 June 1952 at the Tally Ho, North Finchley. (Photo: E. Nicholls)

1960–1969

The shopping habits of the nation were about to change. The supermarket, an idea imported from America, began to dominate the retail trade. The demand was for pre-packed, pre-weighed and pre-priced goods which substantially reduced queuing and the time needed for shopping. It was now possible to do the weekly shopping in one store and pay through the new system of credit cards then being introduced. An important element was the use of colour, graphics and labelling to make the goods more attractive at point of sale.

1970–1979

In spite of considerable controversy over immigration in the years following the war, by this period first-generation immigrants were already well integrated into society. Additionally, many people from Japan and other countries were working in the UK. This class from St Mary's C of E School, then in Hendon Lane, Finchley, reveals the ethnic make-up of an infant class in the Finchley area.

1980–1989

It was in this decade that one of the most intractable problems facing the borough came into focus: road traffic. Traffic jams, parking problems, air pollution and road accidents became more intense, and the frustration and anger caused by delays, poor driving and bad manners even gave rise to a new phrase in the English language: road rage. In spite of high fuel prices, road tax and parking fees, the growth in the number of motor cars has increased and the situation has been made worse by larger lorries and fashionable demands for larger four-wheel-drive vehicles.

1990–2000

It is said that the most significant development in the whole of human history occurred in this decade: the information and communications revolution. The development of the computer and the establishment of international communication networks is still in its infancy but has already led to important social changes such as the elimination of routine office tasks and accounting systems which, in turn, has led to massive reductions in office-type jobs. The future will be in the hands of people such as Christian Brown, featured in this 1999 photograph, whose school syllabus includes computer science and technology.

Index